Pitman Research Notes in Mathematics Series

Submission of proposals for consideration
Suggestions for publication, in the form of outlines and representative samples, are invited by the Editorial Board for assessment. Intending authors should approach one of the main editors or another member of the Editorial Board, citing the relevant AMS subject classifications. Alternatively, outlines may be sent directly to the publisher's offices. Refereeing is by members of the board and other mathematical authorities in the topic concerned, throughout the world.

Preparation of accepted manuscripts
On acceptance of a proposal, the publisher will supply full instructions for the preparation of manuscripts in a form suitable for direct photo-lithographic reproduction. Specially printed grid sheets are provided and a contribution is offered by the publisher towards the cost of typing. Word processor output, subject to the publisher's approval, is also acceptable.

Illustrations should be prepared by the authors, ready for direct reproduction without further improvement. The use of hand-drawn symbols should be avoided wherever possible, in order to maintain maximum clarity of the text.

The publisher will be pleased to give any guidance necessary during the preparation of a typescript, and will be happy to answer any queries.

Important note
In order to avoid later retyping, intending authors are strongly urged not to begin final preparation of a typescript before receiving the publisher's guidelines and special paper. In this way it is hoped to preserve the uniform appearance of the series.

Longman Scientific & Technical
Longman House
Burnt Mill
Harlow, Essex, UK
(tel (0279) 26721)

Longman Scientific & Technical
Churchill Livingstone Inc.
1560 Broadway
New York, NY 10036, USA
(tel (212) 819-5453)

Titles in this series

1 Improperly posed boundary value problems
A Carasso and A P Stone

2 Lie algebras generated by finite dimensional ideals
I N Stewart

3 Bifurcation problems in nonlinear elasticity
R W Dickey

4 Partial differential equations in the complex domain
D L Colton

5 Quasilinear hyperbolic systems and waves
A Jeffrey

6 Solution of boundary value problems by the method of integral operators
D L Colton

7 Taylor expansions and catastrophes
T Poston and I N Stewart

8 Function theoretic methods in differential equations
R P Gilbert and R J Weinacht

9 Differential topology with a view to applications
D R J Chillingworth

10 Characteristic classes of foliations
H V Pittie

11 Stochastic integration and generalized martingales
A U Kussmaul

12 Zeta-functions: An introduction to algebraic geometry
A D Thomas

13 Explicit *a priori* inequalities with applications to boundary value problems
V G Sigillito

14 Nonlinear diffusion
W E Fitzgibbon III and H F Walker

15 Unsolved problems concerning lattice points
J Hammer

16 Edge-colourings of graphs
S Fiorini and R J Wilson

17 Nonlinear analysis and mechanics: Heriot-Watt Symposium Volume I
R J Knops

18 Actions of fine abelian groups
C Kosniowski

19 Closed graph theorems and webbed spaces
M De Wilde

20 Singular perturbation techniques applied to integro-differential equations
H Grabmüller

21 Retarded functional differential equations: A global point of view
S E A Mohammed

22 Multiparameter spectral theory in Hilbert space
B D Sleeman

24 Mathematical modelling techniques
R Aris

25 Singular points of smooth mappings
C G Gibson

26 Nonlinear evolution equations solvable by the spectral transform
F Calogero

27 Nonlinear analysis and mechanics: Heriot-Watt Symposium Volume II
R J Knops

28 Constructive functional analysis
D S Bridges

29 Elongational flows: Aspects of the behaviour of model elasticoviscous fluids
C J S Petrie

30 Nonlinear analysis and mechanics: Heriot-Watt Symposium Volume III
R J Knops

31 Fractional calculus and integral transforms of generalized functions
A C McBride

32 Complex manifold techniques in theoretical physics
D E Lerner and P D Sommers

33 Hilbert's third problem: scissors congruence
C-H Sah

34 Graph theory and combinatorics
R J Wilson

35 The Tricomi equation with applications to the theory of plane transonic flow
A R Manwell

36 Abstract differential equations
S D Zaidman

37 Advances in twistor theory
L P Hughston and R S Ward

38 Operator theory and functional analysis
I Erdelyi

39 Nonlinear analysis and mechanics: Heriot-Watt Symposium Volume IV
R J Knops

40 Singular systems of differential equations
S L Campbell

41 N-dimensional crystallography
R L E Schwarzenberger

42 Nonlinear partial differential equations in physical problems
D Graffi

43 Shifts and periodicity for right invertible operators
D Przeworska-Rolewicz

44 Rings with chain conditions
A W Chatters and C R Hajarnavis

45 Moduli, deformations and classifications of compact complex manifolds
D Sundararaman

46 Nonlinear problems of analysis in geometry and mechanics
M Atteia, D Bancel and I Gumowski

47 Algorithmic methods in optimal control
W A Gruver and E Sachs

48 Abstract Cauchy problems and functional differential equations
F Kappel and W Schappacher

49 Sequence spaces
W H Ruckle

50 Recent contributions to nonlinear partial differential equations
H Berestycki and H Brezis

51 Subnormal operators
J B Conway

52 Wave propagation in viscoelastic media
F Mainardi
53 Nonlinear partial differential equations and their applications: Collège de France Seminar. Volume I
H Brezis and J L Lions
54 Geometry of Coxeter groups
H Hiller
55 Cusps of Gauss mappings
T Banchoff, T Gaffney and C McCrory
56 An approach to algebraic K-theory
A J Berrick
57 Convex analysis and optimization
J-P Aubin and R B Vintner
58 Convex analysis with applications in the differentiation of convex functions
J R Giles
59 Weak and variational methods for moving boundary problems
C M Elliott and J R Ockendon
60 Nonlinear partial differential equations and their applications: Collège de France Seminar. Volume II
H Brezis and J L Lions
61 Singular systems of differential equations II
S L Campbell
62 Rates of convergence in the central limit theorem
Peter Hall
63 Solution of differential equations by means of one-parameter groups
J M Hill
64 Hankel operators on Hilbert space
S C Power
65 Schrödinger-type operators with continuous spectra
M S P Eastham and H Kalf
66 Recent applications of generalized inverses
S L Campbell
67 Riesz and Fredholm theory in Banach algebra
B A Barnes, G J Murphy, M R F Smyth and T T West
68 Evolution equations and their applications
F Kappel and W Schappacher
69 Generalized solutions of Hamilton-Jacobi equations
P L Lions
70 Nonlinear partial differential equations and their applications: Collège de France Seminar. Volume III
H Brezis and J L Lions
71 Spectral theory and wave operators for the Schrödinger equation
A M Berthier
72 Approximation of Hilbert space operators I
D A Herrero
73 Vector valued Nevanlinna Theory
H J W Ziegler
74 Instability, nonexistence and weighted energy methods in fluid dynamics and related theories
B Straughan
75 Local bifurcation and symmetry
A Vanderbauwhede
76 Clifford analysis
F Brackx, R Delanghe and F Sommen
77 Nonlinear equivalence, reduction of PDEs to ODEs and fast convergent numerical methods
E E Rosinger
78 Free boundary problems, theory and applications. Volume I
A Fasano and M Primicerio
79 Free boundary problems, theory and applications. Volume II
A Fasano and M Primicerio
80 Symplectic geometry
A Crumeyrolle and J Grifone
81 An algorithmic analysis of a communication model with retransmission of flawed messages
D M Lucantoni
82 Geometric games and their applications
W H Ruckle
83 Additive groups of rings
S Feigelstock
84 Nonlinear partial differential equations and their applications: Collège de France Seminar. Volume IV
H Brezis and J L Lions
85 Multiplicative functionals on topological algebras
T Husain
86 Hamilton-Jacobi equations in Hilbert spaces
V Barbu and G Da Prato
87 Harmonic maps with symmetry, harmonic morphisms and deformations of metrics
P Baird
88 Similarity solutions of nonlinear partial differential equations
L Dresner
89 Contributions to nonlinear partial differential equations
C Bardos, A Damlamian, J I Díaz and J Hernández
90 Banach and Hilbert spaces of vector-valued functions
J Burbea and P Masani
91 Control and observation of neutral systems
D Salamon
92 Banach bundles, Banach modules and automorphisms of C*-algebras
M J Dupré and R M Gillette
93 Nonlinear partial differential equations and their applications: Collège de France Seminar. Volume V
H Brezis and J L Lions
94 Computer algebra in applied mathematics: an introduction to MACSYMA
R H Rand
95 Advances in nonlinear waves. Volume I
L Debnath
96 FC-groups
M J Tomkinson
97 Topics in relaxation and ellipsoidal methods
M Akgül
98 Analogue of the group algebra for topological semigroups
H Dzinotyiweyi
99 Stochastic functional differential equations
S E A Mohammed

100 Optimal control of variational inequalities
V Barbu
101 Partial differential equations and dynamical systems
W E Fitzgibbon III
102 Approximation of Hilbert space operators. Volume II
C Apostol, L A Fialkow, D A Herrero and D Voiculescu
103 Nondiscrete induction and iterative processes
V Ptak and F-A Potra
104 Analytic functions – growth aspects
O P Juneja and G P Kapoor
105 Theory of Tikhonov regularization for Fredholm equations of the first kind
C W Groetsch
106 Nonlinear partial differential equations and free boundaries. Volume I
J I Díaz
107 Tight and taut immersions of manifolds
T E Cecil and P J Ryan
108 A layering method for viscous, incompressible L_p flows occupying R^n
A Douglis and E B Fabes
109 Nonlinear partial differential equations and their applications: Collège de France Seminar. Volume VI
H Brezis and J L Lions
110 Finite generalized quadrangles
S E Payne and J A Thas
111 Advances in nonlinear waves. Volume II
L Debnath
112 Topics in several complex variables
E Ramírez de Arellano and D Sundararaman
113 Differential equations, flow invariance and applications
N H Pavel
114 Geometrical combinatorics
F C Holroyd and R J Wilson
115 Generators of strongly continuous semigroups
J A van Casteren
116 Growth of algebras and Gelfand–Kirillov dimension
G R Krause and T H Lenagan
117 Theory of bases and cones
P K Kamthan and M Gupta
118 Linear groups and permutations
A R Camina and E A Whelan
119 General Wiener–Hopf factorization methods
F-O Speck
120 Free boundary problems: applications and theory, Volume III
A Bossavit, A Damlamian and M Fremond
121 Free boundary problems: applications and theory, Volume IV
A Bossavit, A Damlamian and M Fremond
122 Nonlinear partial differential equations and their applications: Collège de France Seminar. Volume VII
H Brezis and J L Lions
123 Geometric methods in operator algebras
H Araki and E G Effros
124 Infinite dimensional analysis–stochastic processes
S Albeverio
125 Ennio de Giorgi Colloquium
P Krée
126 Almost-periodic functions in abstract spaces
S Zaidman
127 Nonlinear variational problems
A Marino, L Modica, S Spagnolo and M Degiovanni
128 Second-order systems of partial differential equations in the plane
L K Hua, W Lin and C-Q Wu
129 Asymptotics of high-order ordinary differenti equations
R B Paris and A D Wood
130 Stochastic differential equations
R Wu
131 Differential geometry
L A Cordero
132 Nonlinear differential equations
J K Hale and P Martinez-Amores
133 Approximation theory and applications
S P Singh
134 Near-rings and their links with groups
J D P Meldrum
135 Estimating eigenvalues with *a posteriori/a pri* inequalities
J R Kuttler and V G Sigillito
136 Regular semigroups as extensions
F J Pastijn and M Petrich
137 Representations of rank one Lie groups
D H Collingwood
138 Fractional calculus
G F Roach and A C McBride
139 Hamilton's principle in continuum mechanics
A Bedford
140 Numerical analysis
D F Griffiths and G A Watson
141 Semigroups, theory and applications. Volum
H Brezis, M G Crandall and F Kappel
142 Distribution theorems of L-functions
D Joyner
143 Recent developments in structured continua
D De Kee and P Kaloni
144 Functional analysis and two-point differentia operators
J Locker
145 Numerical methods for partial differential equations
S I Hariharan and T H Moulden
146 Completely bounded maps and dilations
V I Paulsen
147 Harmonic analysis on the Heisenberg nilpote Lie group
W Schempp
148 Contributions to modern calculus of variatio
L Cesari
149 Nonlinear parabolic equations: qualitative properties of solutions
L Boccardo and A Tesei
150 From local times to global geometry, control physics
K D Elworthy

151 A stochastic maximum principle for optimal control of diffusions
U G Haussmann
152 Semigroups, theory and applications. Volume II
H Brezis, M G Crandall and F Kappel
153 A general theory of integration in function spaces
P Muldowney
154 Oakland Conference on partial differential equations and applied mathematics
L R Bragg and J W Dettman
155 Contributions to nonlinear partial differential equations. Volume II
J I Díaz and P L Lions
156 Semigroups of linear operators: an introduction
A C McBride
157 Ordinary and partial differential equations
B D Sleeman and R J Jarvis
158 Hyperbolic equations
F Colombini and M K V Murthy
159 Linear topologies on a ring: an overview
J S Golan
160 Dynamical systems and bifurcation theory
M I Camacho, M J Pacifico and F Takens
161 Branched coverings and algebraic functions
M Namba
162 Perturbation bounds for matrix eigenvalues
R Bhatia
163 Defect minimization in operator equations: theory and applications
R Reemtsen

Defect minimization in operator equations: theory and applications

R Reemtsen

Technical University of Berlin

Defect minimization in operator equations: theory and applications

Longman Scientific & Technical

Copublished in the United States with John Wiley & Sons, Inc., New York

Longman Scientific & Technical
Longman Group UK Limited
Longman House, Burnt Mill, Harlow
Essex CM20 2JE, England
and Associated Companies throughout the world.

Copublished in the United States with
John Wiley & Sons, Inc., 605 Third Avenue, New York, NY 10158

First published 1987

AMS Subject Classifications: (main) 41A65, 47H17
(subsidiary) 34A50, 35A40

ISSN 0269–3674

British Library Cataloguing in Publication Data
Reemtsen, R.
Defect minimization in operator equations:
theory and applications.——— (Pitman research
notes in mathematics series, ISSN 0269–
3674; 163).
1. Operator equations
I. Title
515′.25 QA329
ISBN 0-582-00317-2

Library of Congress Cataloging-in-Publication Data
Reemtsen, R.
Defect minimization in operator equations.

(Pitman research notes in mathematics series,
ISSN 0269–3674 : 163)
Bibliography : p.
1. Operator equations, Nonlinear– Numerical solutions. 2. Approximation theory.
I. Title. II.Series.
QA329.8.R44 1987 515.7′242 87–3789
ISBN 0–470–20877–5 (USA only)

Printed and bound in Great Britain by
Biddles Ltd, Guildford and King's Lynn

MS-SIR
SCIMON

... José Arcadio Buendía spent the long months of the rainy season shut up in a small room that he had built in the rear of the house so that no one would disturb his experiments. Having completely abandoned his domestic obligations, he spent entire nights in the courtyard watching the course of the stars and he almost contracted sunstroke from trying to establish an exact method to ascertain noon. When he became an expert in the use and manipulation of his instruments, he conceived a notion of space that allowed him to navigate across unknown seas, to visit uninhabited territories, and to establish relations with splendid beings without having to leave his study. That was the period in which he acquired the habit of talking to himself, of walking through the house without paying attention to anyone, as Ursula and the children broke their backs in the garden, growing banana and caladium, cassava and yams, ahuyama roots and eggplants. Suddenly, without warning, his feverish activity was interrupted and was replaced by a kind of fascination. He spent several days as if he were bewitched, softly repeating to himself a string of fearful conjectures without giving credit to his own understanding. Finally, one Tuesday in December, at lunchtime, all at once he released the whole weight of his torment. The children would remember for the rest of their lives the august solemnity with which their father, devastated by his prolonged vigil and by the wrath of his imagination, revealed his discovery to them:

"The earth is round, like an orange."...

From "A Hundred Years of Solitude"
by Gabriel Garcia Marquez

Contents

Preface

Many problems in mathematical applications are of the form

$$(P) \quad \text{For } r \in Y \text{ given find } a \in A \text{ such that } Ta = r$$

where T is an operator mapping a nonempty closed subset A of a linear normed space $(X, \|\cdot\|_X)$ into a linear normed space $(Y, \|\cdot\|_Y)$. Provided that (P) possesses a unique solution $\hat{a} \in A$ which depends continuously on the data, a simple method to gain a numerical solution of (P) is to determine any (approximate) solution of the problem

$$(P_n) \quad \text{Minimize } \|r - Ta\|_Y \text{ on } X_n \cap A$$

in which X_n is an appropriate n-dimensional subspace of X generated by $v_1, \ldots, v_n \in X$. If furthermore $\{v_n\}_{n\in\mathbb{N}}$ is a complete family of elements of X such that $\bigcup_{n\in\mathbb{N}} (X_n \cap A)$ is dense in A, a sequence of such problems is obtained, raising the question of the convergence of the method.

This idea, which we have outlined here generally for operator equations, has been employed many times for the numerical solution of specific problems involving differential or integral equations (see the references given in Sections 11 - 13 and OBERG [35], BARRODALE/YOUNG [70], PETSOULAS [75], ATKINSON [76], WIGGINS [78], KRABS [79, 79a], respectively). In these applications the method has usually been justified by a stability estimate of the type

$$\|\hat{a} - a\|_X \le K\|T\hat{a} - Ta\|_Y \quad \text{for all } a \in A \tag{0.1}$$

and/or by a proof of the convergence of solutions of the (P_n) to the solution of (P). However, further theoretical results have rarely been presented, and, what is even more astonishing, the general nature of the method has almost never been emphasized. (BARRODALE and YOUNG [70] discuss the idea of defect minimization for arbitrary linear equations, but primarily with regard to its numerical realization).

These latter observations have motivated us to explore the above approach to the solution of operator equations in general, and this is what we want to do here. In this connection we would like to remark that this particular method has to be carefully distinguished from other methods using complete families (see, for example, HERRERA [84]). So we will only relate to those procedures which are easily seen to be of the above type.

We begin in Sections 1 and 2 with the formulation of the problem and the method, respectively. Sections 3, 4, and 5 are devoted to the questions of the convergence of the method and the existence of a solution to the finite dimensional approximation problem (P_n). Then in Sections 6 and 7 we shall present error estimates and a result on the rate of the convergence. Up to this point we will use relatively simple arguments. Therefore, we would like to point out that we do not intend here to find the weakest possible assumptions, under which the method still works, but rather to provide a simple theoretical framework for this approach.

Section 8 of Chapter 1 can be considered as a contribution to the discretization theory in nonlinear approximation. It is independent of the method studied here, but it fits very well into its context. For, if Y is the space of all real-valued continuous functions on compact $B \subset \mathbb{R}^{\ell}$ and $\|\cdot\|_Y$ is an L_p-norm, (P_n) has to be discretized in order to be solved numerically. This is a fact to which little attention has been payed yet, but which has to be carefully examined, in particular for nonlinear problems.

Thus in Section 8 we shall derive sufficient conditions for the convergence of the minimal values and of solutions of discretized versions of (P_n), where we focus on such conditions which can be actually verified in practice.

We will continue by discussing some further aspects concerning the numerical realization of the solution of (P_n) in Section 9. Finally, in the last section of Chapter 1 we will consider our method in the case of operators which enjoy a certain monotonicity property.

Summarizing we can draw the following conclusions from the results of Chapter 1: In case that T is continuous on A and satisfies a stability estimate of the type (0.1), this estimate ensures the existence of a solution of the finite dimensional approximation problem (P_n) and also in general the 'global convergence' of certain Newton type algorithms for its numerical solution. An estimate of this type is furthermore crucial for the convergence of the method itself and in addition provides a computable error bound in case K is known.

In Chapter 2 we shall apply our previously derived results to some problems governed by differential equations. In order to be specific we will confine ourselves there to a particular choice of the X_n in each case.

We begin in Section 11 with some initial and boundary value problems for ordinary differential equations. For these problems we can fully make use of the results of Chapter 1 where we only have to impose those conditions on the data which entail the unique solvability of the given problem itself.

In Section 12 we shall first discuss the application of the method of defect minimization to the solution of partial differential equations in general and afterwards to the solution of the classical Stefan problem in particular. The idea to employ this approach for the numerical solution of such a free boundary problem has been suggested before by REEMTSEN and LOZANO [81]. These authors have motivated their method by a stability estimate for the free boundary, but have not provided any further analysis of it. In Section 12 we shall verify the convergence of the method and shall moreover be able to apply our results on discretization errors. For that we will essentially only make use of those assumptions which guarantee the existence of a unique classical solution to the given problem itself. Hence the approach designed here for a Stefan problem may be an attractive alternative to traditional methods for the numerical solution of free boundary value problems in general, especially if nonlinear boundary conditions are involved.

Section 13 is concerned with the solution of the so-called inverse Stefan problem. The inverse Stefan problem is 'improperly posed' since it usually does not have a solution or, in case it possesses a solution, this solution does not depend continuously on the data. Hence our primary objective will be to define what we mean by a 'solution' of the problem. At this point diverse approaches leading to operator equations are possible. All these approaches include constraints which regularize the problem, and hence a natural procedure to obtain an approximate solution is to minimize the defect in the corresponding operator equation over a regularizing subset of an appropriate finite dimensional space (cf. also JOCHUM [70, 80] and KNABNER [83a, 85]). The advantage of the approach presented here is that the finite dimensional approximation problems are linear and easily solvable.

In Section 13 we shall summarize in particular the results of REEMTSEN and KIRSCH [84] and COLTON and REEMTSEN [84] on the inverse Stefan problem in one and two space dimensions. In addition, we shall again apply the theorems of Section 8 to the discrete approximation problems and shall furthermore prove, what up to now was only a conjecture, that our special approach does not require any regularizing constraints if the inverse Stefan problem possesses a unique solution and its data are analytic.

In order to prove convergence of the method for the problems in Sections 12 and 13, we shall need stability estimates for the temperature and the free boundary in the classical Stefan problem. We will deduce such estimates (with computable constants) under relatively weak assumptions in the Appendix. We note that the stability of the free boundary in the classical Stefan problem has been proved by other authors before (see e.g. FASANO/PRIMICERIO [77a, b] and KNABNER [83]). However, in contrast to these authors we are able to avoid the use of a certain cumbersome initial transformation.

Chapter 2 provides a theoretical basis for a large number of numerical examples quoted in the mathematical literature. (We shall refer to such examples in each section). The crucial point in the application of the method is the choice of the complete family which generates the subspaces X_n. It determines the rate of convergence of the method and hence should take into consideration as much a priori information on the solution of the given problem as possible. This freedom in the choice of the X_n may be considered as a drawback in one case, but may be used to advantage in other cases in order to produce highly accurate numerical results where traditional traditional methods fail or yield poor results (cf. e.g. BARRODALE/YOUNG [70], COLLATZ/GÜNTHER/SPREKELS [76], and COLTON/REEMTSEN [84]).

At this point I would very much like to thank Prof.Dr. Werner Krabs for his interest in me and my work, his encouragement, and his contagious enthusiasm. To my colleagues Prof.Dr. Johannes Jahn, Dr. Ulrich Lamp, and Dr. Günter Leugering I am grateful for their spirit of friendship and collaboration. Further, I feel obliged to Prof.Dr. Reiner Hettich and to my friends Prof.Dr. David Colton and Prof.Dr. Andreas Kirsch for several fruitful discussions on different parts of this work. Last but not least I thank Mrs. Angelika Garhammer for the excellent typing of the manuscript.

This work is a revised version of my habilitation thesis. I am thankful to Prof.Dr. W. Krabs, Prof.Dr. R. Hettich and Prof.Dr. K. Graf Finck von Finckenstein for having refereed this thesis.

Berlin, West Germany
November 1986

1 Theory

1. THE PROBLEM

Let $(X, \|\cdot\|_X)$ and $(Y, \|\cdot\|_Y)$ be linear normed spaces and let A be a nonempty closed subset of X. Further, let $T : A \subseteq X \to Y$ be an operator which maps $A \subseteq X$ into Y. Then many problems in the mathematical applications are of the following type:

(P) For $r \in Y$ given find $a \in A$ such that $Ta = r$.

Throughout the first part of this book we will study an approach to the numerical solution of (P). We are not interested in the solvability of (P) itself, and hence we will assume if necessary

Assumption A. (P) possesses a unique solution $\hat{a} \in A$.

Obviously, (P) possesses a unique solution for each $r \in Y$ if and only if the inverse operator T^{-1} of T exists.

2. THE METHOD OF MINIMIZING THE DEFECTS

Definition 2.1. T is said to be stable in $a \in A$ if for every $\varepsilon > 0$ there is a $\delta = \delta(\varepsilon) > 0$ so that $\|a - b\|_X < \varepsilon$ holds true for all $b \in A$ for which $\|Ta - Tb\|_Y < \delta$.

We assume now that (P) possesses a unique solution $\hat{a} \in A$ and that T is stable in $\hat{a}$, i.e. that (P) is 'well-posed'. Then a reasonable approach to solve (P) approximately is to choose an appropriate n-dimensional subspace X_n of X and to search for an element $\tilde{a}_n \in (X_n \cap A)$ for which the defect in the operator equation $\|T\hat{a} - T\tilde{a}_n\|_Y = \|r - T\tilde{a}_n\|_Y$ becomes small. For then also a small error $\|\hat{a} - \tilde{a}_n\|_X$ can be expected. Therefore, in order to find an approximate solution of (P), we suggest to solve the finite dimensional minimum norm problem

(P_n) Minimize $\|r - Ta\|_Y$ on $X_n \cap A$.

We define the minimal value of (P_n) by

$$\rho_n = \inf \{\|r - Ta\|_Y | \quad a \in (X_n \cap A)\} \tag{2.1}$$

and say that $\hat{a}_n \in (X_n \cap A)$ is a solution of (P_n) if the infimum in (2.1) is achieved for $\hat{a}_n$.

If we further wish to make ρ_n and $\|\hat{a} - \hat{a}_n\|_X$ (if $\hat{a}_n$ exists) arbitrarily small, we have at least to guarantee that there is a sequence $\{X_n\}_{n\in\mathbb{N}}$ of subspaces X_n of X such that $\hat{a}$ can be approximated by elements of $\bigcup_{n\in\mathbb{N}} (X_n \cap A)$. More precisely, we have to require the following.

<u>Assumption B.</u> There is a family $\{v_n\}_{n\in\mathbb{N}}$ of elements of X such that $\bigcup_{n\in\mathbb{N}} (X_n \cap A)$ is dense in A where $X_n = \langle v_1,\dots,v_n\rangle$ and $\dim X_n = n$.

We note that Assumption B ensures the nonemptiness of $X_n \cap A$ for sufficiently large n.

In order to verify Assumption B, we will normally start from a family of elements in X which is known to be 'complete' in X.

<u>Definition 2.2.</u> A family $\{v_n\}_{n\in\mathbb{N}}$ of elements of X is said to be complete in X if and only if $\bigcup_{n\in\mathbb{N}} X_n$ is dense in X where $X_n = \langle v_1,\dots,v_n\rangle$ and $\dim X_n = n$.

In particular, we can provide the following tool for the verification of Assumption B which we will employ in the applications later on.

<u>Lemma 2.1.</u> Let V be a linear variety in X and $\{X_n\}_{n\in\mathbb{N}}$ be a sequence of n-dimensional subspaces X_n of X such that $\bigcup_{n\in\mathbb{N}} (X_n \cap V)$ is dense in V. If A is a convex subset of V with nonempty interior $\mathring{A}$ relative to V, then $\bigcup_{n\in\mathbb{N}} (X_n \cap A)$ is dense in A.

<u>Proof.</u> We fix a number $\varepsilon > 0$ and an element $a^0 \in \mathring{A}$. Then for every $a \in A$ and every $\delta \in (0,1]$, $a + \delta(a^0 - a)$ is element of $\mathring{A}$ due to the convexity of A. We choose now $\delta_a \in (0,1]$ sufficiently small so that $\delta_a \|a^0 - a\|_X \le \varepsilon/2$. Then we can determine a number $n(a) \in \mathbb{N}$ and an element $a_{n(a)} \in (X_{n(a)} \cap V)$ so that $\|a + \delta_a(a^0 - a) - a_{n(a)}\|_X \le \varepsilon/2$ and $a_{n(a)}$ is in A. Consequently we have

$$\|a - a_{n(a)}\|_X \le \|a + \delta_a(a^0 - a) - a_{n(a)}\|_X + \delta_a \|a^0 - a\|_X \le \varepsilon$$

and $a_{n(a)} \in (X_{n(a)} \cap A)$ which completes the proof. □

3. CONVERGENCE OF THE METHOD

The following theorem answers the question of the convergence of the minimal values ρ_n of (P_n).

Theorem 3.1. Provided that Assumptions A and B are fulfilled and that T is continuous in $\hat{a} \in A$, we have $\lim_{n\to\infty} \rho_n = 0$.

Proof. By virtue of Assumption B, there is a sequence $\{a_n\}_{n\in\mathbb{N}}$ of elements $a_n \in (X_n \cap A)$ such that $\|\hat{a} - a_n\|_X$ tends to zero for $n \to \infty$. Next, continuity of T in $\hat{a} \in A$ implies the convergence of $\|T\hat{a} - Ta_n\|_Y$ to zero for $n \to \infty$. Finally we have $\rho_n \le \|T\hat{a} - Ta_n\|_Y$ such that the proof is complete. □

Hence, under Assumptions A and B there exists a sequence $\{a_n\}_{n\in\mathbb{N}}$ with $a_n \in (X_n \cap A)$ such that $\lim_{n\to\infty} \|T\hat{a} - Ta_n\|_Y = 0$. In particular, if (P_n) possesses a solution $\hat{a}_n \in (X_n \cap A)$ for each $n \in \mathbb{N}$, $\{\hat{a}_n\}_{n\in\mathbb{N}}$ is such a sequence. If we further wish to guarantee the convergence of $\hat{a}_n$ to $\hat{a}$ in X, we have to assume that T is stable in $\hat{a} \in A$.

In practice, stability of the operator is often established by an estimate of the type (0.1) together with the existence of a solution of the operator equation (cf. also Sects. 6 and 7). Therefore, we give here only the following trivial theorem.

Theorem 3.2. Let the inverse T^{-1} of T exist. Then T^{-1} is continuous in Ta for $a \in A$ if and only if T is stable in $a \in A$.

4. THE INVERSE BOUNDEDNESS CONDITION

Before we will turn to the question of the existence of a solution to (P_n), we want to study a property of certain operators, the so-called 'inverse boundedness'. In practice, the attempt of verifying the inverse boundedness of T is often the only chance to possibly ensure the solvability of (P_n) (as well as the global convergence of algorithms for the numerical solution of (P_n) (cf. Sect. 9)).

Definition 4.1. An operator $T : A \subseteq X \to Y$ is said to be bounded on A if every bounded subset $S \subseteq A$ has a bounded image T(S) under T.

Correspondingly we define 'inverse boundedness' of T (cf. REEMTSEN [80]).

Definition 4.2. We say that $T : A \subseteq X \to Y$ is inversely bounded on $S \subseteq A$ if for every $\alpha \geq 0$ the level set

$$C_\alpha(S) = \{a \in S \mid \|Ta\|_Y \leq \alpha\} \qquad (4.1)$$

is bounded.

The following example shows that the assumption of the inverse boundedness of T is in general quite restrictive if T is a nonlinear operator.

Example 4.1. Let $A = X = \mathbb{R}$ and let $Y = C[1,2]$ where $\|\cdot\|_Y$ is the supremum norm on [1,2]. Further, let $T : A \to Y$ be defined by $(Ta)(x) = 1/(1+a^2x)$ for $a \in A$ and $x \in [1,2]$. Then $C_\alpha(A)$ is unbounded for every $\alpha > 0$. □

However, the approach of Sect. 2 is only reasonable if T is a stable operator, and for stable operators inverse boundedness can often be guaranteed as the following lemma states.

Lemma 4.1. Let there exist an $\bar{a} \in A$ and a constant $K > 0$ such that T is stable in $\bar{a} \in A$ in the sense that

$$\|\bar{a} - a\|_X \leq K\|T\bar{a} - Ta\|_Y \quad \text{for all } a \in A. \qquad (4.2)$$

Then T is inversely bounded on A.

Proof. Let $a \in A$ be such that $\|Ta\|_Y \leq \alpha$ for $\alpha \geq 0$. Then by (4.2) we have

$$\|a\|_X \leq K(\|T\bar{a}\|_Y + \alpha) + \|\bar{a}\|_X. \qquad \square$$

We conclude this section by studying the relationship between inverse boundedness of T and the existence of the inverse operator T^{-1} of T.

Lemma 4.2. If T^{-1} exists and is bounded on $T(A) = Y$, then T is inversely bounded on A.

The proof of Lemma 4.2 follows readily from Definitions 4.1 and 4.2. Furthermore, if T is a linear operator, also the converse of Lemma 4.2 holds true for certain subsets $A \subseteq X$.

Lemma 4.3. Let T be a linear mapping from $A \subseteq X$ onto Y where A is a convex cone with vertex at the origin. Then the following conditions are equivalent:

(1) $C_\alpha(A)$ (4.1) is bounded for a single $\alpha > 0$.

(2) T is inversely bounded on A.

(3) T^{-1} exists and is bounded on $T(A)$.

Proof. Let condition (1) hold true. Then $C_\beta(A)$ is bounded for all β with $0 \le \beta \le \alpha$. In case $\beta = \gamma\alpha$ and $\gamma > 1$, for all $a \in C_\beta(A)$, a/γ is in $C_\alpha(A)$. Hence there is a constant η so that $\|a\|_X \le \eta\gamma$. Thus condition (1) implies (2).

Now let T be inversely bounded on A. Then we have $C_0(A) = \{0\}$ since A is a convex cone with vertex at the origin. Therefore, the inverse T^{-1} of T exists. Furthermore, by definition inverse boundedness of T on A implies boundedness of T^{-1} on $T(A)$. Hence (3) holds true. Finally, condition (3) implies (1) by Lemma (4.2). □

If T is a nonlinear operator, T may be inversely bounded on A, but may not have an inverse T^{-1}. This situation occurs, for example, if $A = X = \mathbb{R}$, $Y = \{r \in \mathbb{R} \mid r \ge 0\}$, and $Ta = a^2$.

5. EXISTENCE OF SOLUTIONS TO (P_n)

This section is devoted to the question of the solvability of the finite dimensional minimum norm problem (P_n). For that we fix $a_0 \in (X_n \cap A)$, if $X_n \cap A$ is nonempty, and define

$$\beta_0 = \|r - Ta_0\|_Y + \|r\|_Y. \tag{5.1}$$

Moreover, we set

$$C_\alpha(X_n \cap A) = \{a \in (X_n \cap A) \mid \|Ta\|_Y \leq \alpha\} \tag{5.2}$$

for $\alpha \geq 0$ (cf. (4.1)). Then we first observe the following (see YOUNG [07]).

Lemma 5.1. $\rho_n = \inf\{\|r - Ta\|_Y \mid a \in C_{\beta_0}(X_n \cap A)\}$
where β_0 is given by (5.1). Furthermore, if $\hat{a}_n \in (X_n \cap A)$ is a solution of (P_n), $\hat{a}_n$ is in $C_{\beta_0}(X_n \cap A)$.

Proof. $\rho_n = \inf\{\|r - Ta\|_Y \mid a \in (X_n \cap A) \text{ and } \|r - Ta\|_Y \leq \|r - Ta_0\|_Y\}$
$\geq \inf\{\|r - Ta\|_Y \mid a \in (X_n \cap A) \text{ and } \|Ta\|_Y \leq \beta_0\} \geq \rho_n$.
From these inequalities we can also conclude that a solution $\hat{a}_n$ of (P_n) is in $C_{\beta_0}(X_n \cap A)$ if it exists. □

Making use of Lemma 5.1, we can now prove the following existence theorem.

Theorem 5.1. If the image $T(X_n \cap A)$ of $X_n \cap A$ under T is a closed subset of a finite dimensional subspace of Y, (P_n) possesses a solution $\hat{a}_n \in (X_n \cap A)$.

Proof. By the assumptions of the theorem, the set

$$\{Ta \in T(X_n \cap A) \mid \|Ta\|_Y \leq \beta_0\}$$

with β_0 (5.1) is compact. Hence the existence of a solution to (P_n) follows from Lemma 5.1 and WEIERSTRASS' theorem. □

For linear operators T, Theorem 5.1 ensures the solvability of (P_n) in many circumstances. So, in particular, (P_n) possesses a solution if A is a linear variety in X or if A is the solution set of finitely many linear inequalities. (In the second case the closedness of $T(X_n \cap A)$ is due to the fact that A is 'finitely generated' (see ROCKAFELLAR [72])). If, however, the range of T is not closed, (P_n) may not have a solution as the following example demonstrates.

Example 5.1. Let $X_n = \mathbb{R}^2$ and $Y = C[0,1]$ where Y is equipped with the supremum norm on [0,1]. Further, let $T : X_n \to Y$ be defined by

$$(Ta)(x) = (a_1 - a_2)x, \quad x \in [0,1].$$

Then we consider (P_n) for $r = 0$ in Y and

$$A = \{(a_1,a_2) \in \mathbb{R}^2 \mid \; a_1 \geq 1, \; 0 \leq a_2 \leq \sqrt{a_1^2 - 1}\}.$$

We note that A is a closed convex set and hence is the intersection of the closed half-spaces which contain it (see ROCKAFELLAR [72]). Thus (P_n) can here be interpreted as a 'semi-infinite linear programming problem' (cf. HETTICH/ZENCKE [82]).

Obviously, for all $(a_1,a_2) \in A$ we have now $a_1 \geq a_2$ so that

$$\rho_n = \inf_{(a_1,a_2)\in A} \; \max_{x\in[0,1]} |(Ta)(x)| = \inf_{(a_1,a_2)\in A} (a_1 - a_2)$$
$$= \inf_{a_1 \geq 1} (a_1 - \sqrt{a_1^2-1}) = 0 \tag{5.3}$$

where the infimum in (5.3) is not achieved for any $a_1 \geq 1$. □

If T is nonlinear, the assumptions of Theorem 5.1 are usually not fulfilled. Therefore, we provide another simple existence theorem which can be successfully applied in many situations (see also YOUNG [07]).

Theorem 5.2. If T is continuous on $X_n \cap A$ and if $C_{\beta_0}(X_n \cap A)$ (5.2) with β_0 (5.1) is bounded, then (P_n) possesses a solution $\hat{a}_n \in (X_n \cap A)$.

Proof. The continuity of T on $X_n \cap A$ implies the continuity of the mapping $a \to \|Ta\|_Y$ from $X_n \cap A$ into $\mathbb{R}$. Thus $C_{\beta_0}(X_n \cap A)$ is a closed and hence a compact set. So by Lemma 5.1 there is an element $\hat{a}_n \in (X_n \cap A)$ which solves (P_n). □

From Theorem 5.2 and Lemma 4.1 we can deduce the following conclusion which is essential in view of the method of Sect. 2.

<u>Conclusion 5.1.</u> Let T be continuous on A. Further, let there exist an element $\bar{a} \in A$ and a constant K so that (4.2) holds true. Then (P_n) has a solution $\hat{a}_n \in (X_n \cap A)$.

Furthermore, applying Lemma 4.2 we arrive at the following result.

<u>Conclusion 5.2.</u> Provided that T is continuous on A and that T^{-1} exists and is bounded on T(A) = Y, (P_n) possesses a solution $\hat{a}_n \in (X_n \cap A)$.

Other existence theorems for the solution of (P_n) in abstract spaces can be found in the book by FISHER and JEROME [75]. Moreover, for some special sets of functions $T(X_n \cap A)$, proofs of existence can be found in the textbooks of approximation theory (e.g. see COLLATZ/KRABS [73] on rational and exponential approximation).

We finally would like to remark that the question of the uniqueness of a solution to (P_n) depends strongly on the norm of Y.

6. ERROR BOUNDS

It is one advantage of the method suggested in Sect. 2 that for a solution $\hat{a}_n$ of (P_n) (if it exists) the error in the data $\|T\hat{a} - T\hat{a}_n\|_Y$ is given by ρ_n directly and that the error $\|\hat{a} - \hat{a}_n\|_X$ can be computed easily in many situations. More precisely, we can say the following.

<u>Remark 6.1.</u> Let Assumption A be fulfilled.

(1) If T is Lipschitz continuous on A with constant K_1, then

$$K_1^{-1} \|r - Ta\|_Y \le \|\hat{a} - a\|_X \quad \text{for all } a \in A.$$

(2) If there is a stability constant K_2 such that

$$\|\hat{a} - a\|_X \le K_2 \|T\hat{a} - Ta\|_Y \quad \text{for all } a \in A, \tag{6.1}$$

then this inequality yields an upper bound for $\|\hat{a} - a\|_X$ where $\|T\hat{a} - Ta\|_Y = \|r - Ta\|_Y$.

Moreover, recalling Conclusion 5.1, we arrive at the following.

Conclusion 6.1. Let all assumptions of Remark 6.1 be satisfied. Then (P_n) possesses a solution $\hat{a}_n \in (X_n \cap A)$ and

$$K_1^{-1} \rho_n \le \|\hat{a} - \hat{a}_n\|_X \le K_2 \rho_n.$$

7. ON THE RATE OF CONVERGENCE

Concerning the rate of convergence of solutions of (P_n) to the solution of (P) for $n \to \infty$, we can easily derive the following result.

Theorem 7.1. Let Assumption A be fulfilled and let $\tilde{a}_n$ be an element of $X_n \cap A$ such that

$$\|\hat{a} - \tilde{a}_n\|_X = \min \{\|\hat{a} - a\|_X \mid a \in (X_n \cap A)\}. \tag{7.1}$$

Further, let T be Lipschitz continuous on A with constant K_1. Then we have:

(1) $\rho_n \le K_1 \|\hat{a} - \tilde{a}_n\|_X$.

(2) If in addition there is a constant K_2 such that (6.1) holds true for $\hat{a} \in A$, (P_n) has a solution $\hat{a}_n \in (X_n \cap A)$ and $\|\hat{a} - \hat{a}_n\|_X \le K_1 K_2 \|\hat{a} - \tilde{a}_n\|_X$.

Proof. (1) is true because of

$$\rho_n \le \|r - T\tilde{a}_n\|_Y \le K_1 \|\hat{a} - \tilde{a}_n\|_X.$$

Then (2) is a consequence of statement (1) and Conclusion 6.1. □

Thus we can conclude from Theorem 7.1 that under Assumption B, ρ_n and $\|\hat{a} - \hat{a}_n\|_X$ tend to zero for $n \to \infty$ as fast as $\hat{a} \in A$ can be approximated by elements of $(X_n \cap A)$ in X. Hence for the method under consideration it is of interest to obtain results on the rate of the convergence of (7.1) for $n \to \infty$. There are only few such results known to us. We refer in particular to the well-known theorems of JACKSON which provide such qualitative statements for the case that $X = A = C[c,d]$ and X_n is the space of all polynomials on the interval $[c,d]$ with degree at most $n - 1$ (cf. CHENEY [66]).

8. DISCRETIZATION OF (P_n) IN CASE Y = C(B)

Let $1 \le p \le \infty$ and $B \subset \mathbb{R}^\ell$ be a compact set; in particular, let $B = [c,d]$ if $1 \le p < \infty$. Further, let C(B) be the space of all real-valued continuous functions on B. Then in this section we consider (P_n) for the special case that Y = C(B) and

$$\|f\|_Y := \|f\|_B = \begin{cases} \max\limits_{\xi\in B} |f(\xi)| & \text{if } p = \infty, \\ \{\int_c^d |f(\xi)|^p\}^{1/p} & \text{if } 1 \le p < \infty. \end{cases} \tag{8.1}$$

In practice, it is usually impossible to solve (P_n) directly. Therefore, in order to handle (P_n) numerically, one will try to 'simplify' the problem through discretization in the following sense.

Let $B_k \subseteq B$ be compact. In particular, for $1 \le p < \infty$ let B_k consist of k points $\xi_i^{(k)} \in \mathbb{R}$, $1 \le i \le k$, with

$$c \le \xi_1^{(k)} < \xi_2^{(k)} < \dots < \xi_k^{(k)} \le d$$

where $\xi_i^{(k)} \in [y_{i-1}^{(k)}, y_i^{(k)}]$ and the $y_i^{(k)}$ are such that $y_{i-1}^{(k)} < y_i^{(k)}$ and

$$[c,d] = [y_0^{(k)}, y_1^{(k)}] \cup [y_1^{(k)}, y_2^{(k)}] \cup \dots \cup [y_{k-1}^{(k)}, y_k^{(k)}].$$

Then setting

$$h_i^{(k)} = y_i^{(k)} - y_{i-1}^{(k)}, \quad 1 \le i \le k,$$

we define the discrete semi-norm corresponding to (8.1) by

$$\|f\|_{B_k} = \begin{cases} \max\limits_{\xi\in B_k} |f(\xi)| & \text{if } p = \infty, \\ \{\sum\limits_{i=1}^{k} |f(\xi_i^{(k)})|^p\, h_i^{(k)}\}^{1/p} & \text{if } 1 \le p < \infty. \end{cases}$$

We assume further that A_k is a closed upper set of A in X and that the domain of T can be extended to $X_n \cap A_k$. (Note that the domain of T is varying in this section whereas the range of T is always in $C(B) \subseteq C(B_k)$). So if, for example, A is the solution set of infinitely many linear constraints, A_k may be the solution set of finitely many of them. Then instead of (P_n), one will try to solve the problem

$$(P_n^k) \quad \text{Minimize } \|r - Ta\|_{B_k} \quad \text{on } X_n \cap A_k.$$

In correspondence with (2.1), we set

$$\rho_n^k = \inf \{\|r - Ta\|_{B_k} \mid a \in (X_n \cap A_k)\}$$

and call $\hat{a}_n^k \in (X_n \cap A_k)$ a solution of (P_n^k) if the infimum is achieved for $\hat{a}_n^k$.

A question of obvious interest is now: provided that $\{B_k\}_{k\in\mathbb{N}}$ and $\{A_k\}_{k\in\mathbb{N}}$ are sequences which in an appropriate way converge to B and A, respectively, do the ρ_n^k tend to ρ_n for $k \to \infty$ if n is fixed? (We note that n is fixed throughout this section, i.e. we consider (P_n) independently of (P). Thus, in particular, we will not make use of Assumptions A and B here).

It is well-known that the above question can be answered in the affirmative, if T is linear and, for example, $A = A_k = X$ (see WATSON [80]). Furthermore, it has been shown that there are nonlinear problems where the ρ_n^k do not converge to ρ_n (see DUNHAM [72] and the examples below). This is disturbing in view of the fact that almost all algorithms for the solution of approximation problems, including those for the solution of semi-infinite programming problems (cf. HETTICH/ZENCKE [82]), are based on discretization. Hence it is of big practical importance to identify such operators T for which the requested convergence can be shown.

For linear unconstrained L_∞-problems, i.e. if T is linear, $A = A_k = X$, and $p = \infty$, the problem of the convergence of the discretization errors has been studied first by CHENEY [66]. WATSON [80] gives a corresponding proof for $p = 1$ which can be easily transferred to the case $1 < p < \infty$. Moreover, results on the rate of convergence have been obtained by CHALMERS [78] for $p = \infty$ and by KROÓ [81] for $p = 1$. Finally, for linear problems which are equivalent to certain semi-infinite programming problems a convergence result of the requested type can be found in the book by HETTICH and

ZENCKE [82].

Concerning discrete nonlinear approximations, almost exclusively exponential and rational approximation problems have been investigated so far (cf. BRAESS [73], BURKE [76], KRABS [73b], LOEB/WOLFE [73], WOLFE [75, 77, 79]). However, it has been noted that the discretization of approximation problems can be considered as a special perturbation problem in optimization and hence can be tackled with the available theories in this connection (see e.g. KRABS [73a]). We shall discuss the relation of our results to this latter approach in Remark 8.1 (2) below. Our aim here is to derive sufficient conditions for the convergence of the ρ_n^k to ρ_n which can be actually verified in many circumstances.

We begin by giving some definitions. For $T : S \subseteq X \to C(B)$ and $\alpha \geq 0$ we set

$$C_\alpha(S) = \{a \in S \mid \|Ta\|_B \leq \alpha\}$$

(cf. (4.1)) and correspondingly

$$C_\alpha^k(S) = \{a \in S \mid \|Ta\|_{B_k} \leq \alpha\}.$$

Further, assuming the nonemptiness of $X_n \cap A$, we fix some $a_0 \in (X_n \cap A)$ and a number $\sigma > 0$ (where also $\sigma = 0$ is possible for $p = \infty$) and define

$$\alpha_0 = \|r - Ta_0\|_B + \|r\|_B + \sigma. \tag{8.2}$$

Moreover, for M and Q being nonempty subsets of a linear normed space $(Z, \|\cdot\|_Z)$ we write

$$h(M,Q) = \sup_{x \in Q} \inf_{y \in M} \|x - y\|_Z.$$

Hence we have $\lim_{k\to\infty} h(M, M_k) = 0$, where $\{M_k\}_{k\in\mathbb{N}}$ is a sequence of nonempty subsets of Z, if and only if for each $\varepsilon > 0$ there is a number $k(\varepsilon) \in \mathbb{N}$ such that for all $k \geq k(\varepsilon)$

$$M_k \subseteq M_\varepsilon = \{x \in Z \mid \inf_{y \in M} \|x - y\|_Z \leq \varepsilon\}.$$

We can now state the following two general assumptions of this section.

Assumption 8.1. $\{B_k\}_{k\in\mathbb{N}}$ is a sequence of compact subsets of B in $(\mathbb{R}^\ell, \|\cdot\|_2)$ such that $\lim_{k\to\infty} h(B_k, B) = 0$ where $\|\cdot\|_2$ is the Euclidean norm.

Assumption 8.2. $\{A_k\}_{k\in\mathbb{N}}$ is a sequence of closed subsets of $(X, \|\cdot\|_X)$ where (for nonempty $A \subseteq X$)

(i) $A \subseteq \ldots \subseteq A_{k+1} \subseteq A_k \subseteq \ldots \subseteq A_1 \subseteq X$.

Further, if $X_n \cap A$ is nonempty, we have either

(ii) $\lim_{k\to\infty} h(X_n \cap A, X_n \cap A_k) = 0$ or,

(ii)' provided that T maps $X_n \cap A_{\hat{k}}$ into C(B) for a $\hat{k} = \hat{k}(n) \in \mathbb{N}$,

$$\lim_{k\to\infty} h(C_{\alpha_0}(X_n \cap A), C^k_{\alpha_0}(X_n \cap A_k)) = 0.$$

In applications, Assumption 8.2 (ii)' may be satisfied because of the possible boundedness of the level sets $C_{\alpha_0}(X_n \cap A)$ and $C^k_{\alpha_0}(X_n \cap A_k)$ while at the same time (ii) may not hold true. We also note that Assumption 8.2 is always fulfilled if $A = A_k$ for all $k \in \mathbb{N}$.

Finally, we provide the following result.

Lemma 8.1. (1) $\rho_n = \inf\{\|r - Ta\|_B \mid a \in C_{\alpha_0}(X_n \cap A)\}$.

If $\hat{a}_n \in (X_n \cap A)$ is a solution of (P_n), $\hat{a}_n$ is element of $C_{\alpha_0}(X_n \cap A)$.

(2) Let Assumptions 8.1 and 8.2 (i) hold true and let T be a mapping from $X_n \cap A_{\hat{k}}$ into C(B) for a $\hat{k} = \hat{k}(n) \in \mathbb{N}$. Then there is a number $k_0 \geq \hat{k}$, where $k_0 = \hat{k}$ if $p = \infty$, such that for all $k \geq k_0$

$$\rho^k_n = \inf\{\|r - Ta\|_{B_k} \mid a \in C^k_{\alpha_0}(X_n \cap A_k)\}.$$

Further, if $\hat{a}^k_n \in (X_n \cap A_k)$ solves (P^k_n), $k \geq k_0$, $\hat{a}^k_n$ is in $C^k_{\alpha_0}(X_n \cap A_k)$.

Proof. Statement (1) is a consequence of Lemma 5.1. Now let $k \geq \hat{k}$. Then by virtue of Assumption 8.2 (i), $a_0 \in (X_n \cap A)$ is element of $X_n \cap A_k$. Hence we have

$$\rho_n^k \geq \inf \{\|r - Ta\|_{B_k} \mid a \in (X_n \cap A_k) \text{ and } \|Ta\|_{B_k} \leq \|r - Ta_0\|_{B_k} + \|r\|_{B_k}\}.$$

If $p = \infty$,

$$\|r - Ta_0\|_{B_k} + \|r\|_{B_k} \leq \alpha_0 \tag{8.3}$$

for all $k \geq \hat{k}$ is obvious. In case $1 \leq p < \infty$, (8.3) is true for all sufficiently large k by the definition of the Riemann integral. Then the remainder of the proof follows the proof of Lemma 5.1. □

For $T : X_n \cap A_{\hat{k}} \to C(B)$ and $\{A_k\}_{k \in \mathbb{N}}$ as in Assumption 8.2 (i), let now

$$N = \bigcup_{k \geq \hat{k}} C_{\alpha_0}^k (X_n \cap A_k)$$

and

$$N_\varepsilon = \{a \in X \mid \ \|a - b\|_X \leq \varepsilon \quad \text{for a } b \in N\} \tag{8.4}$$

be an ε-neighborhood of N in X. (Obviously, N is a subset of $X_n \cap A_{\hat{k}}$). Then in the following we shall give the main theorem of this section. Afterwards we will study its assumptions for specific situations.

Theorem 8.1. Let Assumptions 8.1 and 8.2 be fulfilled and let $T : X_n \cap A_{\hat{k}} \to C(B)$ be continuous on $X_n \cap A_{\hat{k}}$ for a $\hat{k} = \hat{k}(n) \in \mathbb{N}$. Moreover, let T be uniformly continuous on $N_{\hat{\varepsilon}} \cap (X_n \cap A_{\hat{k}})$ for an $\hat{\varepsilon} > 0$ in case $A \neq A_k$ for some $k \geq \hat{k}$. Finally, let (P_n^k) have a solution $\hat{a}_n^k \in (X_n \cap A_k)$ for each $k \geq \hat{k}$ and let $\{T\hat{a}_n^k\}_{k \geq \hat{k}}$ be equicontinuous on B. Then we have:

(1) $\lim_{k \to \infty} \rho_n^k = \rho_n$.

(2) $\lim_{k \to \infty} \|r - T\hat{a}_n^k\|_B = \rho_n$.

If in addition there is a constant C so that $\|\hat{a}_n^k\|_X \leq C$ for all $k \geq \hat{k}$, then also the following holds true:

(3) $\{\hat{a}_n^k\}_{k \geq \hat{k}}$ possesses at least one accumulation point which lies in $X_n \cap A$ and each such accumulation point solves (P_n).

(4) If moreover (P_n) has a unique solution $\hat{a}_n \in (X_n \cap A)$, then $\lim_{k\to\infty} \|\hat{a}_n - \hat{a}_n^k\|_X = 0$.

<u>Proof.</u> (1). With respect to Assumption 8.2 we define either

$$M = X_n \cap A \quad \text{and} \quad M_k = X_n \cap A_k,$$

particularly if $A = A_k$ for all $k \geq \hat{k}$, or

$$M = C_{\alpha_0}(X_n \cap A) \quad \text{and} \quad M_k = C_{\alpha_0}^k(X_n \cap A_k).$$

In any case M and M_k, $k \geq \hat{k}$, are nonempty sets. Let further for $\varepsilon \in (0,\hat{\varepsilon}]$

$$\Delta(\varepsilon) = \begin{cases} 0, & \text{if } A = A_k \text{ for all } k \geq \hat{k}, \\ \sup\{\|Ta-Tb\|_B \mid \|a-b\|_X \leq \varepsilon,\ a,\ b \in N_{\hat{\varepsilon}} \cap (X_n \cap A_{\hat{k}})\}, & \text{else.} \end{cases}$$

Obviously, we have $\Delta(\varepsilon) \to 0$ for $\varepsilon \to 0$.

In the following let $\varepsilon \in (0,\hat{\varepsilon}]$ be fixed.

We first observe that by Lemma 8.1 there is a number $k_0 \geq \hat{k}$ such that $\hat{a}_n^k$ is in $C_{\alpha_0}^k(X_n \cap A_k) \subseteq M_k$ if $k \geq k_0$. Further, by virtue of Assumption 8.2, there exists a number $k_1 \geq \hat{k}$ such that we have $M_k \subseteq M_\varepsilon$ for all $k \geq k_1$. Hence, if $k \geq \max(k_0,k_1)$, we can find an element $\tilde{a}_k \in M$ with $\|\tilde{a}_k - \hat{a}_n^k\|_X \leq \varepsilon$. In particular, we can choose $\tilde{a}_k = \hat{a}_n^k$ if $A = A_k$ for all $k \geq \hat{k}$.

We next note that in any case $M \subseteq (X_n \cap A) \subseteq (X_n \cap A_{\hat{k}})$ holds true. Therefore, we can infer that $\hat{a}_n^k$ as well as $\tilde{a}_k$ belong to $N_{\hat{\varepsilon}} \cap (X_n \cap A_{\hat{k}})$ for each $k \geq \max(k_0,k_1)$. Thus, if $k \geq \max(k_0,k_1)$, we have

$$\inf_{a \in (X_n \cap A)} \|r - Ta\|_B - \|r - T\hat{a}_n^k\|_B \leq \|r - T\tilde{a}_k\|_B - \|r - T\hat{a}_n^k\|_B \leq \Delta(\varepsilon). \tag{8.5}$$

Our next objective is now to study the expression

$$\|r - T\hat{a}_n^k\|_B - \inf_{a\in(X_n\cap A_k)} \|r - Ta\|_{B_k} = \|r - T\hat{a}_n^k\|_B - \|r - T\hat{a}_n^k\|_{B_k}. \tag{8.6}$$

For $f \in C(B)$ we define

$$\omega(f,\varepsilon) = \sup \{|f(x) - f(y)| \mid \|x-y\|_2 \le \varepsilon, \ \ x, y \in B\} \tag{8.7}$$

to be the modulus of continuity of f on B. Then we set

$$\mu_n(\varepsilon) = \sup_{k\ge\hat{k}} \omega(T\hat{a}_n^k,\varepsilon), \tag{8.8}$$

and we observe that $\mu_n(\varepsilon)$ tends to zero with $\varepsilon \to 0$ because of the equicontinuity of $\{T\hat{a}_n^k\}_{k\ge\hat{k}}$ on B. Further, due to Assumption 8.1, there is a number $k_2 \ge \hat{k}$ so that $h(B_k,B) \le \varepsilon$ for all $k \ge k_2$. Let now $k \ge k_2$ and let first $1 \le p < \infty$. Then choose $\theta_i^{(k)} \in B$ such that

$$|r(\theta_i^{(k)}) - (T\hat{a}_n^k)(\theta_i^{(k)})| = \max_{y_{i-1}^{(k)}\le x\le y_i^{(k)}} |r(x) - (T\hat{a}_n^k)(x)|.$$

Hence, we have $\|\xi_i^{(k)} - \theta_i^{(k)}\|_2 \le \varepsilon$ for all i, $1 \le i \le k$. If we use now

$$\|r - T\hat{a}_n^k\|_B^p = \sum_{i=1}^k \int_{y_{i-1}^{(k)}}^{y_i^{(k)}} |r(x) - (T\hat{a}_n^k)(x)|^p \, dx$$

$$\le \sum_{i=1}^k |r(\theta_i^{(k)}) - (T\hat{a}_n^k)(\theta_i^{(k)})|^p \, h_i^{(k)}$$

and apply Minkowski's inequality twice, we can derive

$$\|r - T\hat{a}_n^k\|_B - \|r - T\hat{a}_n^k\|_{B_k}$$

$$\le \{ \sum_{i=1}^k |[r(\theta_i^{(k)}) - (T\hat{a}_n^k)(\theta_i^{(k)})] - [r(\xi_i^{(k)}) - (T\hat{a}_n^k)(\xi_i^{(k)})]|^p \, h_i^{(k)}\}^{1/p}$$

$$\le \{ \sum_{i=1}^k |r(\theta_i^{(k)}) - r(\xi_i^{(k)})|^p \, h_i^{(k)}\}^{1/p}$$

$$+ \{ \sum_{i=1}^{k} |(T\hat{a}_n^k)(\theta_i^{(k)}) - (T\hat{a}_n^k)(\xi_i^{(k)})|^p \, h_i^{(k)}\}^{1/p}$$

$$\leq K\{\omega(r,\varepsilon) + \mu_n(\varepsilon)\} \tag{8.9}$$

where $K = (d-c)^{1/p}$. In case $p = \infty$, (8.9) is easily seen to be true for $K = 1$.

Combining (8.5), (8.6), and (8.9), we get for $1 \leq p \leq \infty$ and $k \geq \max(k_0,k_1,k_2)$

$$\inf_{a \in (X_n \cap A)} \|r - Ta\|_B - \inf_{a \in (X_n \cap A_k)} \|r - Ta\|_{B_k} \leq \Delta(\varepsilon) + K\{\omega(r,\varepsilon) + \mu_n(\varepsilon)\}. \tag{8.10}$$

By virtue of our assumptions, the right-hand side of (8.10) tends to zero with $\varepsilon \to 0$.

For $p = \infty$, it is easily seen that the left-hand side of (8.10) is always nonnegative since we have $B_k \subseteq B$ and $A \subseteq A_k$. Thus, statement (1) is verified in this case.

If $1 \leq p < \infty$, for every $a \in (X_n \cap A)$ there is a number $E(a,h^{(k)})$, where $h^{(k)} = \max_{1 \leq i \leq k} h_i^{(k)}$, so that we have $E(a,h^{(k)}) \to 0$ for $h^{(k)} \to 0$ and

$$\{\int_c^d |r(x) - (Ta)(x)|^p \, dx\}^{1/p} =$$

$$= \{\sum_{i=1}^{k} |r(\xi_i^{(k)}) - (Ta)(\xi_i^{(k)})|^p \, h_i^{(k)}\}^{1/p} + E(a,h^{(k)}).$$

We note that $h^{(k)}$ tends to zero if and only if $h(B_k,B)$ does so. Now we choose $b \in (X_n \cap A)$ so that $\|r - Tb\|_B - \inf_{a \in (X_n \cap A)} \|r - Ta\|_B < \varepsilon$. Then there exists a $k_3 \geq \hat{k}$ such that $|E(b,h^{(k)})| \leq \varepsilon$ for all $k \geq k_3$. Hence

$$\rho_n + \varepsilon \geq \|r - Tb\|_{B_k} + E(b,h^{(k)}) \geq \rho_n^k - \varepsilon, \quad k \geq k_3. \tag{8.11}$$

Combination of (8.10) and (8.11) yields the requested result.

(2). From 8.5 we can conclude that

$$\rho_n - \rho_n^k - \Delta(\varepsilon) \le \|r - T\hat{a}_n^k\|_B - \|r - T\hat{a}_n^k\|_{B_k} \tag{8.12}$$

for all $k \ge \max(k_0, k_1)$ holds true, and from (8.9) and (8.12) we obtain recalling (1)

$$\lim_{k\to\infty} \left| \|r - T\hat{a}_n^k\|_B - \|r - T\hat{a}_n^k\|_{B_k} \right| = 0. \tag{8.13}$$

Finally we write

$$|\rho_n - \|r - T\hat{a}_n^k\|_B| \le |\rho_n - \rho_n^k| + \left| \|r - T\hat{a}_n^k\|_{B_k} - \|r - T\hat{a}_n^k\|_B \right|,$$

so that statement (2) follows from (1) and (8.13).

(3). By our assumption all $\hat{a}_n^k$, $k \ge \hat{k}$, are elements of the compact set $\{a \in X_n | \ \|a\|_X \le C\}$. Hence there exists a subsequence $\{\hat{a}_n^{k(i)}\}_{i\in\mathbb{N}}$ of $\{\hat{a}_n^k\}_{k\ge\hat{k}}$ which converges to an element $\bar{a}_n \in X_n$. Since for all sufficiently large i $\hat{a}_n^{k(i)}$ is in $M_{k(i)}$ (cf. Lemma 8.1) and M is a closed set due to the continuity of T, we can easily conclude from Assumption 8.2 that $\bar{a}_n$ has to be element of M. Furthermore, the continuity of T on $X_n \cap A_{\hat{k}}$ implies that $\|r - T\hat{a}_n^{k(i)}\|_B$ tends to $\|r - T\bar{a}_n\|_B$ for $i \to \infty$. Consequently, from (2) we get that $\bar{a}_n$ is a solution of (P_n).

(4). If in addition (P_n) possesses a unique solution $\hat{a}_n \in (X_n \cap A)$, then every convergent subsequence of $\{\hat{a}_n^k\}_{k\ge\hat{k}}$ and thus the whole sequence converges to $\hat{a}_n$. □

<u>Remarks 8.1.</u> (1) It can be easily verified that in case of Assumption 8.2 (ii)', Theorem 8.1 (as well as Lemma 8.2) remains true if $N_{\hat{\varepsilon}} \cap (X_n \cap A_{\hat{k}})$ is replaced by $\bigcup_{k\ge\hat{k}} C^k_{\alpha_0}(X_n \cap A_k) \cup C_{\alpha_0}(X_n \cap A)$.

(2). If (P_n) is considered as a special optimization problem and (P_n^k) as a corresponding problem with perturbed data, the questions of this section can be attacked with the perturbation theories in optimization. However, as we shall show, little is gained by such an approach since the verification of the assumptions of these theories for our problem requires most of the arguments of the proofs presented here.

Let us first relate to the results of KRABS [73]. We can fit the problems (P_n) and (P_n^k) into the model considered by KRABS if we choose the parameters there as follows:

$$E := \bigcup_{k \geq \hat{k}} C^k_{\alpha_0}(X_n \cap A_k) \cup C_{\alpha_0}(X_n \cap A) \quad \text{(equipped with } \|\cdot\|_X),$$

$$X := C_{\alpha_0}(X_n \cap A), \quad S := X, \quad f(x) := \|r - Tx\|_B,$$

$$X_k := C^k_{\alpha_0}(X_n \cap A_k), \quad S_k := X_k, \quad f_k(x) := \|r - Tx\|_{B_k},$$

where we suppose that Assumptions 8.1, 8.2 (i) and (ii)' are fulfilled and T is continuous on $X_n \cap A_{\hat{k}}$. Then Satz 3.1 by KRABS [73] shows first that for the proof of Theorem 8.1 (1) the assumptions of the existence of the $\hat{a}_n^k$ and the equicontinuity of $\{T\hat{a}_n^k\}_{k \geq \hat{k}}$ on B can be replaced by the 'uniform equicontinuity of the f_k on E' and condition (3.1) ebd. However, if we wish to establish this equicontinuity of the f_k here for nonlinear T, we will assume the compactness of E (which implies the existence of the $\hat{a}_n^k$ (cf. Lemmas 8.1 and 8.2)) and will, moreover, have to verify condition (3.3) in KRABS [73] (see Lemma 3.2 ebd.). The proof of this latter condition can be accomplished with arguments similar to those which we needed above for the proof of Theorem 8.1 (1). The reader may further confirm that in case T is linear (where the assumption of the compactness of E is usually too strong) the proof of the assumptions of Satz 3.1 requires similar estimates as we shall derive them in the proof of Theorem 8.2 below.

Corresponding considerations can be carried through for the theorem of KRABS [73a]. (We also note that condition (1.1) there can only be fulfilled if $p = \infty$).

Furthermore, KRABS [77] summarizes a large number of results in parametric optimization by using the concept of set-valued mappings. But again the verification of the assumptions of the corresponding theorems for our problem necessitates the same boundedness and equicontinuity assumptions which we referred to above (cf. condition (2.2) there).

(3). One may ask if there is a connection between our results here and the quite general theories developed by STUMMEL [73], VAINIKKO [76], et. al. for the discretization of operator equations. As far as we can see, such a connection is evident only in the special case where T is linear, $p = 2$, and $A = X_n$, i.e. where (P_n) and (P_n^k) are equivalent to the solution of the so-called normal equations (e.g. see WATSON [80]). In that case, after a suitable choice of the parameters, convergence of $\{\hat{a}_n^k\}_{k \geq \hat{k}}$ can also be derived from the theorem on p. 50 in the book of VAINIKKO, provided that (P_n) possesses a unique solution. However, we would like to remark that we conclude this latter fact from the convergence of the minimal values $\{\rho_n^k\}_{k \geq \hat{k}}$, which can be proved without the assumption of the unique solvability of (P_n) (cf. Theorem 8.1 in connection with Theorem 8.2).

8.1. LINEAR OPERATORS

If T is a linear operator, the existence of solutions to (P_n) and (P_n^k) can often be ensured with simple arguments. In particular, (P_n) and (P_n^k) possess solutions if $A = X$ and T is the identical operator (cf. Theorem 5.1). Hence, in combination with Theorem 8.1, the following theorem extends results of CHENEY [66] and WATSON [80] for $p = \infty$ and $1 \leq p < \infty$, respectively.

Theorem 8.2. Let Assumptions 8.1 and 8.2 (i) be fulfilled and let T be a linear map from X_n into $C(B)$. Further, let (P_n^k) have a solution $\hat{a}_n^k \in (X_n \cap A_k)$ for each $k \geq \hat{k}$. Then the following is true:

(1) $\{T\hat{a}_n^k\}_{k \geq \hat{k}}$ is equicontinuous on B.

(2) If $\dim T(X_n) = n$, there is a constant C so that $\|\hat{a}_n^k\|_X \leq C$ for all $k \geq \hat{k}$.

Proof. (1). Let $w_i = Tv_i$, $1 \leq i \leq n$, if $X_n = \langle v_1, \ldots, v_n \rangle$, and let the first $m \leq n$ of the w_i be linearly independent. Further, for $\varepsilon > 0$ we define

$$\Omega_m(\varepsilon) = \max_{1 \leq i \leq m} \omega(w_i, \varepsilon)$$

with ω (8.7). Obviously, $\Omega_m(\varepsilon)$ tends to zero for $\varepsilon \to 0$. Then, if $T\hat{a}_n^k = \sum_{i=1}^{m} \beta_i^k w_i$ and $\|x - y\|_2 \leq \varepsilon$, we obtain

$$|(T\hat{a}_n^k)(x) - (T\hat{a}_n^k)(y)| \leq \|\beta^k\|_1 \, \Omega_m(\varepsilon)$$

where $\|\cdot\|_1$ is the ℓ_1-norm in $\mathbb{R}^m$. Hence the proof of (1) is complete if there is a constant M such that $\|\beta^k\|_1 \le M$ for all $k \ge \hat{k}$.

For that we define

$$\theta_m = \min_{\|\beta\|_1=1} \| \sum_{i=1}^{m} \beta_i w_i \|_B .$$

Due to the linear independence of the w_i, we have $\theta_m > 0$. Next we choose $\varepsilon > 0$ sufficiently small so that $\Omega_m(\varepsilon) \le \theta_m/[2K]$ with K from (8.9). Then there is a number $k_1 \ge \hat{k}$ so that $h(B_k, B) \le \varepsilon$ for all $k \ge k_1$. If we make use of (8.9) for $r = 0$, we finally get for all $k \ge k_1$

$$\theta_m \|\beta^k\|_1 \le \| \sum_{i=1}^{m} \beta_i^k w_i \|_B \le K\,\Omega_m(\varepsilon)\, \|\beta^k\|_1 + \| \sum_{i=1}^{m} \beta_i^k w_i \|_{B_k}$$

$$\le \frac{\theta_m}{2} \|\beta^k\|_1 + \| \sum_{i=1}^{m} \beta_i^k w_i \|_{B_k} .$$

Therefore, by Lemma 8.1 we have for all $k \ge \max(k_0, k_1)$

$$\|\beta^k\|_1 \le \frac{2}{\theta_m} \| \sum_{i=1}^{m} \beta_i^k w_i \|_{B_k} \le \frac{2\alpha_0}{\theta_m} . \tag{8.14}$$

(2). Let now $\hat{a}_n^k = \sum_{i=1}^{n} \gamma_i^k v_i$. Then in the proof of (1) we have $m = n$ and $\beta_i^k = \gamma_i^k$, $1 \le i \le n$, so that (2) is a consequence of (8.14). □

<u>Remark 8.2.</u> Let $A = X$, $X_n = \langle v_1, \dots, v_n \rangle$, T be linear, and $Tv_1, \dots, Tv_n$ be linearly independent. Then, if $1 < p < \infty$, (P_n) always possesses a unique solution. For $p = 1$ or $p = \infty$, it is well-known that a solution of (P_n) is unique if $Tv_1, \dots, Tv_n$ form a so-called 'Haar system' on B (see e.g. WATSON [80]).

8.2. NONLINEAR OPERATORS

If T is a nonlinear operator, in general the existence of solutions to (P_n) and (P_n^k) is difficult to verify, not to speak of the uniqueness of solutions. In 8.2.1 we shall provide a condition which for $p = \infty$ guarantees the existence of solutions $\hat{a}_n \in (X_n \cap A)$ and $\hat{a}_n^k \in (X_n \cap A_k)$ and in many situations also the equicontinuity of $\{T\hat{a}_n^k\}_{k\geq\hat{k}}$. Afterwards in 8.2.2, we shall study this condition for the case $1 \leq p < \infty$.

8.2.1. THE CASE $p = \infty$

Throughout this subsection we assume that $p = \infty$. Then we can state the following lemma concerning the assumptions of Theorem 8.1.

Lemma 8.2. Let Assumptions 8.1 and 8.2 (i) be satisfied and let in addition

$$B_k \subseteq B_{k+1} \subseteq \ldots \subseteq B, \quad k \in \mathbb{N}. \tag{8.15}$$

Further, let there exist a number $\hat{k} = \hat{k}(n) \in \mathbb{N}$ such that $T : X_n \cap A_{\hat{k}} \to C(B)$ is continuous on $X_n \cap A_{\hat{k}}$ and $C_{\alpha_0}^{\hat{k}}(X_n \cap A_{\hat{k}})$ is bounded. Then

(1) (P_n) and (P_n^k), $k \geq \hat{k}$, have solutions $\hat{a}_n \in (X_n \cap A)$ and $\hat{a}_n^k \in (X_n \cap A_k)$, respectively.

(2) T is uniformly continuous on $N_\varepsilon \cap (X_n \cap A_{\hat{k}})$ for each $\varepsilon > 0$ with N_ε defined by (8.4).

(3) There is a constant C such that $\|\hat{a}_n^k\|_X \leq C$ for all $k \geq \hat{k}$.

Proof. Due to our assumptions

$$C_{\alpha_0}(X_n \cap A) \subseteq \ldots \subseteq C_{\alpha_0}^{k+1}(X_n \cap A_{k+1}) \subseteq C_{\alpha_0}^{k}(X_n \cap A_k) \tag{8.16}$$

holds true for $k \in \mathbb{N}$. Hence $C_{\alpha_0}(X_n \cap A)$ and $C_{\alpha_0}^k(X_n \cap A_k)$, $k \geq \hat{k}$, are bounded and by the continuity of T also closed sets in X. So, recalling Lemma 8.1, we can establish (1).

Finally, (2) and (3) follow from the fact that (8.16) implies

$$\bigcup_{k\geq\hat{k}} C_{\alpha_0}^k(X_n \cap A_k) = C_{\alpha_0}^{\hat{k}}(X_n \cap A_{\hat{k}})$$

and hence $N_\varepsilon \cap (X_n \cap A_{\hat{k}})$ is a compact set for each $\varepsilon > 0$. □

In many situations statement (3) of Lemma 8.2 ensures the equicontinuity of $\{T\hat{a}_n^k\}_{k\geq\hat{k}}$ on B. Moreover, (8.16) exhibits that boundedness of $C_{\alpha_0}^{\hat{k}}(X_n \cap A_{\hat{k}})$ for a $\hat{k} \in \mathbb{N}$ guarantees boundedness of $C_{\alpha_0}(X_n \cap A)$. Unfortunately, in practice $C_{\alpha_0}(X_n \cap A)$ can be easier examined than $C_{\alpha_0}^{\hat{k}}(X_n \cap A_{\hat{k}})$ (see e.g. Lemma 4.1). However, boundedness of $C_{\alpha_0}(X_n \cap A)$ does not necessarily imply boundedness of $C_{\alpha_0}^{\hat{k}}(X_n \cap A_{\hat{k}})$ as we shall demonstrate by the following example. This example proves in addition that the uniform approximation problem can have a solution while at the same time none of the discrete problems possesses one (see also DUNHAM [72] for another example).

Example 8.1. Let $A = X_n = \mathbb{R}$, $B = [0,1]$, $r = 0$ on B, and let $T : X_n \to C(B)$ be defined by

$$(Ta)(x) = (1+a^2)e^{-a^2x}, \quad a \in \mathbb{R}.$$

Then because of

$$\max_{x\in B} |(Ta)(x)| = 1 + a^2,$$

$C_\alpha(A)$ is bounded for every $\alpha > 1$, and $\inf_{a\in\mathbb{R}} \|Ta\|_B = 1$ is uniquely achieved for $a = 0$.

If we define now $B_k = [\varepsilon_k, 1]$ where $\{\varepsilon_k\}_{k\geq 0}$ is a nonincreasing sequence of positive reals which converges to zero, then we have

$$\max_{x\in B_k} |(Ta)(x)| = (1+a^2)e^{-a^2\varepsilon_k}.$$

Hence none of the $C_\alpha^k(A)$ is bounded. Besides, $\inf_{a\in\mathbb{R}} \|Ta\|_{B_k} = 0$ is not attained for any $a \in \mathbb{R}$. □

Example 8.1 suggests imposing additional constraints on the parameters in order to avoid numerical difficulties.

Remark 8.3. So far we have considered the case that the range of T is in C(B). However, we will often encounter the situation that $T = (T_1,\ldots,T_q)^t$ where T_i maps A into $C(B^{(i)})$ and the $B^{(i)}$, $1 \leq i \leq q$, are compact subsets of

$\mathbb{R}^\ell$. In this case, T is a mapping from A into the product space $C(B^{(1)}) \times \ldots \times C(B^{(q)})$ which we supply with the norm

$$|||r|||_B = \max_{1 \le i \le q} \|r_i\|_{B^{(i)}}, \quad r_i \in C(B^{(i)}),$$

where $\|\cdot\|_{B^{(i)}}$ is the sup-norm on $B^{(i)}$.

For every $i \in \{1,\ldots,q\}$ let now $\{B_k^{(i)}\}_{k \in \mathbb{N}}$ be a sequence of sets which fulfills Assumption 8.1 and let

$$|||r|||_{B_k} = \max_{1 \le i \le q} \|r_i\|_{B_k^{(i)}}, \; k \in \mathbb{N}.$$

Further, let $r_i \in C(B^{(i)})$, $1 \le i \le q$, be given and let us consider (P_n) and (P_n^k) with the two-bar norms being replaced by the three-bar norms. Then if we substitute $|||\cdot|||_B$ and $|||\cdot|||_{B_k}$ for $\|\cdot\|_B$ and $\|\cdot\|_{B_k}$ throughout the preceding part of this section and if we further require those conditions which we above assumed for T for all components T_i of T here, Theorems 8.1 and 8.2 as well as Lemmas 8.1 and 8.2 remain valid.

8.2.2. THE CASE $1 \le p < \infty$

Let us first demonstrate that a similar situation as in Example 8.1 for $p = \infty$ can arise if $1 \le p < \infty$.

Example 8.2. Let T be defined as in Example 8.1, but choose $p = 1$ here. Then for all $a \neq 0$ we compute

$$\|Ta\|_B = \int_0^1 (1+a^2)e^{-a^2x}\, dx = (1+a^{-2})(1-e^{-a^2}) > 1.$$

Hence $\inf_{a \in \mathbb{R}} \|Ta\|_B = 1$ is uniquely achieved for $a = 0$. If now $0 < \xi_1^{(k)} < \xi_2^{(k)} < \ldots < \xi_k^{(k)} \le 1$, we get

$$k(1+a^2)e^{-a^2\xi_1^{(k)}} \max_{1 \le i \le k} h_i^{(k)} \ge \sum_{i=1}^{k} |(Ta)(\xi_i^{(k)})|\, h_i^{(k)} = \|Ta\|_{B_k}$$

$$\geq k(1+a^2)e^{-a^2\xi_k^{(k)}} \min_{1\leq i\leq k} h_i^{(k)}$$

$$\geq k(1+a^2)e^{-a^2} \min_{1\leq i\leq k} h_i^{(k)}.$$

Thus, for fixed k, $\|Ta\|_{B_k}$ tends to zero for $|a|\to\infty$. Therefore, none of the $C_\alpha^k(A)$ is bounded and $\inf_{a\in\mathbb{R}} \|Ta\|_{B_k} = 0$ is not achieved for any $a\in\mathbb{R}$. □

Moreover, the following example shows that, opposite to the case $p=\infty$, for $1\leq p<\infty$ all of the $C_\alpha^k(X_n\cap A_k)$ may be bounded (which implies the existence of solutions to the discrete problems) while simultaneously $C_\alpha(X_n\cap A)$ is unbounded for every $\alpha>0$ (and the uniform problem has no solution).

<u>Example 8.3.</u> We assume again $A = X_n = \mathbb{R}$, $B = [0,1]$, and $p = 1$. In addition we define $r = 0$ on B and $T : X_n \to C(B)$ by

$$(Ta)(x) = (1+a^2)/(1+a^4x), \quad a\in\mathbb{R}.$$

Then for $a\neq 0$ we have

$$\|Ta\|_B = \int_0^1 \frac{1+a^2}{1+a^4x}\,dx = \frac{1+a^2}{a^4}\log(1+a^4)$$

which tends to zero for $|a|\to\infty$. Hence $\inf_{a\in\mathbb{R}} \|Ta\|_B = 0$, where the infimum is not achieved for any $a\in\mathbb{R}$.

Further, if $0 = \xi_1^{(k)} < \xi_2^{(k)} < \ldots < \xi_k^{(k)} \leq 1$, we obtain

$$\|Ta\|_{B_k} = \sum_{i=1}^{k} |(Ta)(\xi_i^{(k)})|\, h_i^{(k)} \geq h_1^{(k)}(1+a^2).$$

Consequently, for fixed k, $\|Ta\|_{B_k}$ tends to infinity for $|a|\to\infty$. Therefore, all $C_\alpha^k(A)$ are bounded . Moreover, since T is continuous with respect to the L_∞-norm, all $C_\alpha^k(A)$ are closed, and hence all discrete problems possess solutions (use Theorem 5.2 with $Y = C(B_k)$). It is not seen here whether the ρ_n^k converge to ρ_n or not. □

Thus for $1 \le p < \infty$ a result corresponding to Lemma 8.2 cannot be expected. However, we can obtain some insight into the situation here if we relate the level sets $C_\alpha(X_n \cap A)$ and $C_\alpha^k(X_n \cap A_k)$ for C(B) supplied with an L_p-norm, $1 \le p < \infty$, to the corresponding sets where C(B) is associated with the supremum norm. For that matter we write here $\|\cdot\|_{B,p}$ and $\|\cdot\|_{B_k,p}$ instead of $\|\cdot\|_B$ and $\|\cdot\|_{B_k}$ and rename $C_\alpha(S)$ and $C_\alpha^k(S)$ by $C_\alpha^p(S)$ and $C_\alpha^{k,p}(S)$ in order to mark that the (semi-) norm on C(B) equals $\|.\|_{B,p}$ and $\|.\|_{B_k,p}$, respectively.

Then we can state the following lemma.

Lemma 8.3. Let T be defined on $S \subset X$, $B = [c,d]$, and $1 \le p < \infty$. Then we have

(1) $C_\alpha^1(S) \supseteq C^p_{\alpha/(d-c)^{1-1/p}}(S) \supseteq C^\infty_{\alpha/(d-c)}(S)$.

(2) $C_\alpha^{k,1}(S) \supseteq C^{k,p}_{\alpha/(d-c)^{1-1/p}}(S) \supseteq C^{k,\infty}_{\alpha/(d-c)}(S)$.

(3) $C_\alpha^{k,\infty}(S) \supseteq C^{k,1}_{\alpha\mu^{(k)}}(S) \supseteq C^{k,p}_{\alpha\mu^{(k)}/(d-c)^{1-1/p}}(S)$ where

$$\mu^{(k)} = \min_{1\le i\le k} h_i^{(k)}. \tag{8.17}$$

Proof. For $v \in C[c,d]$ we have by Hölder's inequality

$$\|v\|_{B,1} = \int_c^d |v(x)\cdot 1|\,dx \le \|v\|_{B,p}\,\|1\|_{B,p/(p-1)} =$$

$$= \|v\|_{B,p}\,(d-c)^{1-1/p} \le \|v\|_{B,\infty}\,(d-c)$$

which yields (1). Similarly we obtain

$$\|v\|_{B_k,1} = \sum_{i=1}^k |v(\xi_i^{(k)})h_i^{(k)1/p}\,h_i^{(k)(p-1)/p}| \le \|v\|_{B_k,p}\{\sum_{i=1}^k h_i^{(k)}\}^{(p-1)/p}$$

$$= \|v\|_{B_k,p}(d-c)^{1-1/p} \le \|v\|_{B_k,\infty}(d-c) \tag{8.18}$$

and hence we can derive (2). Finally, with $|v(\xi_r^{(k)})| = \max_{1\le i\le k} |v(\xi_i^{(k)})|$ we arrive at

$$\|v\|_{B_k,\infty}\cdot\mu^{(k)} = |v(\xi_r^{(k)})|\,\mu^{(k)} \le \sum_{i=1}^{k} |v(\xi_i^{(k)})|\,h_i^{(k)} = \|v\|_{B_k,1}$$

which together with (8.18) implies (3). □

Using previous arguments (cf. Lemma 8.2), we can draw the following conclusions from Lemma 8.3.

Conclusions 8.1. (1) Let $B = [c,d]$ and T be continuous on $X_n \cap A$ with respect to $\|\cdot\|_{B,\infty}$ on $C(B)$. If $C_{\hat{\alpha}}^{1}(X_n \cap A)$ is bounded for $\hat{\alpha} = \alpha_0 \max(1, d-c)$ with α_0 (8.2), then (P_n) has a solution $\hat{a}_n \in (X_n \cap A)$ for all p, $1 \le p \le \infty$.

(2) Let $B = [c,d]$ and let Assumptions 8.1 and 8.2 (i) be fulfilled. Moreover, let (8.15) hold true and let T be continuous on $X_n \cap A_{\hat{k}}$ for $\hat{k} = \hat{k}(n) \in \mathbb{N}$ with respect to $\|\cdot\|_{B,\infty}$ on $C(B)$. If there is further a number $k_0 \ge \hat{k}$ such that $C_\alpha^{k_0,\infty}(X_n \cap A_{k_0})$ is bounded for all $\alpha \ge 0$, then (P_n^k) possesses a solution $\hat{a}_n^k \in (X_n \cap A_k)$ for each p, $1 \le p \le \infty$, and each $k \ge k_0$.

9. NUMERICAL ASPECTS OF THE METHOD FOR THE CASE Y = C(B)

We continue by making some comments which concern the numerical solution of (P_n) and (P_n^k) for the particular situation given in Sect. 8. The following first remark refers to the use of algorithms.

Remark 9.1. Let $\{a_i\}_{i\ge 0}$ be a sequence of elements in $X_n \cap A$ such that

$$\|r - Ta_{i+1}\|_B \le \|r - Ta_i\|_B \quad \text{for all } i \ge 0. \tag{9.1}$$

Then all a_i, $i \ge 0$, lie in the level set $C_{\alpha_0}(X_n \cap A)$ where the first element a_0 of $\{a_i\}_{i\ge 0}$ determines (8.2).

Correspondingly, if $p = \infty$ and $\{a_i\}_{i\ge 0}$ is a sequence in $X_n \cap A_k$ which satisfies

$$\|r - Ta_{i+1}\|_{B_k} \le \|r - Ta_i\|_{B_k} \quad \text{for all } i \ge 0, \tag{9.2}$$

then all a_i, $i \ge 0$, belong to $C_{\alpha_0}^{k}(X_n \cap A_k)$. (Use Lemma 8.1 for a similar result in case $1 \le p < \infty$).

Analogous statements hold true for the situation discussed in Remark 8.3.

REEMTSEN [82] studied the global convergence of a class of algorithms for the solution of nonlinear approximation problems (see also the survey article by SCHABACK [84] and the quantitative results for this type of algorithms in SCHABACK [85]). The algorithms of this class generate a sequence of iterates $\{a_i\}_{i \ge 0}$ which suffices (9.1) (or (9.2)) and 'converges' to a critical point of (P_n) (or (P_n^k)) provided that T is Fréchet differentiable on A and all a_i, $i \ge 0$, are embedded into a compact set. According to Remark 9.1, the latter assumption is satisfied if $C_{\alpha_0}(X_n \cap A)$ (or $C^k_{\alpha_0}(X_n \cap A_k)$) is compact.

We note here that for all nonlinear problems in this book we will prove the compactness of the corresponding level sets. Hence we can guarantee the 'global convergence' of a whole class of algorithms for the numerical solution of these problems.

Further, we can generally say the following with regard to the method suggested in Sect. 2. It is characteristic for this method that it yields approximate solutions in a closed form and that for such solutions computable error bounds can be provided in many circumstances (cf. Conclusion 6.1 which also justifies to solve (P_n^k) instead of (P_n) as long as the assumptions of Theorem 8.1 are fulfilled). Moreover, the method becomes numerically very efficient if an (approximate) solution $\tilde{a}_n$ of (P_n) (or (P_n^k)) is chosen as an initial guess for the solution of a higher dimensional problem. (For, if $m \ge n$, we have $\rho_m \le \|r - T\tilde{a}_n\|_B$ or $\rho_m^k \le \|r - T\tilde{a}_n^k\|_{B_k}$, respectively). Thus the method can be arranged in such a way that all previously computed data can be fully used to advantage.

10. MONOTONE OPERATORS

In order to compute an error bound for an approximate solution of (P), a stability constant K_2 as in (6.1) has to be determined explicitly. For a certain class of operators, error estimates can be obtained in another more direct way.

Definition 10.1. Let $(W, \|\cdot\|_W)$ and $(Y, \|\cdot\|_Y)$ be partially ordered normed spaces and let A be a nonempty subset of W. Then $T : A \subseteq W \to Y$ is said to be of monotone kind if $Tw_1 \le Tw_2$ implies $w_1 \le w_2$ for $w_1, w_2 \in A$ (cf. COLLATZ [66]).

In the following discussion let X_n be an n-dimensional subspace of W. Then one possibility to take advantage of the monotonicity of an operator T is to solve the defect minimization problem (P_n) with X = W and A being replaced by

$$A^{(1)} = \{a \in A \mid Ta - r \ge 0 \text{ in } Y\}. \tag{10.1}$$

For then a solution $\hat{a}_n^{(1)} \in (X_n \cap A^{(1)})$ of (P_n) (if it exists) satisfies

$$\hat{a}_n^{(1)} \ge \hat{a}, \tag{10.2}$$

provided that Assumption A is fulfilled (cf. COLLATZ [52]). Similarly we can obtain a lower bound $\hat{a}_n^{(2)}$ of $\hat{a}$ if we substitute

$$A^{(2)} = \{a \in A \mid Ta - r \le 0 \text{ in } Y\} \tag{10.3}$$

for $A^{(1)}$ in the above program.

Both problems fit our model problem (P) and hence can be attacked with the theory developed before. Thus, in particular stability of T in $\hat{a}$ has to be required if convergence of the $\hat{a}_n^{(1)}$ (or/and the $\hat{a}_n^{(2)}$) to $\hat{a}$ shall be guaranteed (see also Remarks 10.1 below).

An alternative approach, which makes use of the monotonicity of an operator T, is the following:

(O_{2n}) Minimize $\|a^{(1)} - a^{(2)}\|_W$ over all $(a^{(1)}, a^{(2)}) \in (X_n \cap A^{(1)}) \times (X_n \cap A^{(2)})$

where $A^{(1)}$ and $A^{(2)}$ are defined by (10.1) and (10.3). Then any solution $(\tilde{a}_n^{(1)}, \tilde{a}_n^{(2)}) \in (X_n \cap A^{(1)}) \times (X_n \cap A^{(2)})$ of (O_{2n}) (if it exists) provides 'optimal' bounds

$$\tilde{a}_n^{(1)} \le \hat{a} \le \tilde{a}_n^{(2)}. \tag{10.4}$$

We notice here that if, for example, $\|\cdot\|_W$ is the usual supremum norm on [a,b], the objective function $\|a^{(1)} - a^{(2)}\|_W$ in (O_{2n}) can be exchanged for the function

$$\sup_{x\in[a,b]} [a^{(2)}(x) - a^{(1)}(x)] \tag{10.5}$$

(cf. COLLATZ/KRABS [73], COLLATZ [80]).

Monotonicity, which often reflects the principle of action and reaction in a physical process, has been proved for a large number of operators. It has furthermore been used for the solution of problems in one or the other way described above (see e.g. COLLATZ [52, 66, 80], COLLATZ/GÜNTHER/SPREKELS [76], GROTHKOPF [81], KRABS [79]). Therefore, it seems to us to be worthwhile to study the finite dimensional problems (O_{2n}) in a similar way as we have studied the problems (P_n) before. However, in this connection we like to make the following remarks.

Remarks 10.1. (1) In most applications W has been a subspace of C(B) where W has often been supplied with a norm which entails the discontinuity of T on $A \subseteq W$. (E.g. for the second order boundary value problem of Sect. 11.3 here, monotonicity was shown by KRABS [79], p. 146, where KRABS chose W to be the space $C^2[a,b]$ with $\|\cdot\|_W$ being the maximum norm on [a,b]. However, in order to derive convergence results in this case, we should equip the space $C^2[a,b]$ with the norm $\|\cdot\|_X$ of Sect. 11 below. But note that if we do this we cannot exchange $\|a^{(1)} - a^{(2)}\|_W$ in (O_{2n}) for (10.5) any more).

Moreover, the applications given in the literature show that the above two approaches usually provide (one-sided) error bounds with respect to the maximum norm whereas in the same situations the method developed here yields error bounds in a stronger norm. (E.g. compare the examples of Sect. 11 with similar ones in COLLATZ [52, 80] and KRABS [79]).

(2) If convergence of the $\hat{a}_n^{(1)}$ and $\hat{a}_n^{(2)}$ (or of the $\tilde{a}_n^{(1)}$ and $\tilde{a}_n^{(2)}$, respectively) shall be proved, it has to be shown that $\bigcup_{n\in\mathbb{N}} (X_n \cap A^{(1)})$ lies dense in $A^{(1)}$ and $\bigcup_{n\in\mathbb{N}} (X_n \cap A^{(2)})$ lies dense in $A^{(2)}$. Even if Assumption B is fulfilled , this turns out to be a difficult task if T is a nonlinear operator. In addition, for such a proof most likely also stability of T has to be assumed.

(3) If, for example, Y = C(B), a difficulty arising in practice is to guarantee that the inequalities in $A^{(1)}$ and $A^{(2)}$ are really satisfied on

all of B, which is necessary in order to arrive at (10.2) and (10.4). For note that we have e.g. $T\hat{a}_n^{(1)} - r \approx 0$ on B for sufficiently large n, if $\hat{a}_n^{(1)}$ tends to $\hat{a}$.

2 Applications

11. ORDINARY DIFFERENTIAL EQUATIONS

In the case of ordinary differential equations, the idea of minimizing the defect in the differential equation over a subset of a finite dimensional space has been given by a large number of authors where normally the maximum norm has been used. We would like to start here with reviewing this earlier work.

YOUNG [07] studied the existence of solutions to Chebyshev approximation problems. He applied his theory to an approximation problem which consists in minimizing the defect in an n-th order linear ordinary differential equation with constant coefficients, and he thereby showed that this problem possesses a unique polynomial solution.

McEWEN [31], who refers to earlier work of KRYLOFF and KRAWTCHOUK, proved for linear n-th order boundary value problems with nonconstant coefficients that the finite dimensional defect minimization problems possess solutions with respect to an L_p-norm, $1 \le p < \infty$. He further showed that in case of algebraic or trigonometric polynomials these solutions converge uniformly to the solution of the boundary value problem, and he also provided results on the rate of this convergence. Later on McEWEN's results have been extended by STEIN and KLOPFENSTEIN [68].

SCHMIDT and WIGGINS [79] give a detailed analysis of the method of defect minimization for a linear second order boundary value problem (see also Sect. 11.1 below). Motivated by the paper of SCHMIDT and WIGGINS [79], BOGAR and JEPPSON [80] refer (without proofs) to similar results for linear systems with boundary conditions. Let us finally mention that in case of linear problems numerical work has also been done by KRABS (cf. RABINOWITZ [68]) and BARRODALE and YOUNG [70].

HUFFSTUTLER and STEIN [68a,b] and BACOPOULOS and KARTSATOS [72] study defect minimization for the first order initial value problem $y' = f(x,y)$, $y(a) = \gamma$, and prove uniform convergence of polynomial solutions of the finite dimensional minimization problems for certain functions f.

With regard to nonlinear initial and boundary value problems of second order, research has been done by HENRY, KRABS, and WIGGINS. In particular, HENRY [69, 70] generalizes results of HUFFSTUTLER and STEIN [68a], and HENRY [73] shows existence and convergence of discrete solutions to the problem considered by HENRY [70]. (As REEMTSEN [87] has shown, the assumptions of HENRY [70, 73] also allow the direct application of our discretization theory in Sect. 8). Further, HENRY and WIGGINS [76] describe a related alternative procedure for solving the general second order initial value problem. Let us finally mention that KRABS [79], p. 150, derived an error bound of the type (6.1) for a boundary value problem of second order which enables us to reach furthergoing results on this problem here (see Sect. 11.3).

The idea of defect minimization has also been employed for the numerical solution of differential equations with deviating arguments by ALLINGER and HENRY [76] and HENRY and WIGGINS [78, 81]. It has furthermore been exploited for integro-differential equations by KARTSATOS and SAFF [73] and WIGGINS [79].

In the following subsections we will systematically apply our previously obtained results to some initial and boundary value problems. In each case we will write the problem under consideration in the form of our model problem (P). For that we generally set $X = C^q[a,b]$ and

$$\|y\|_X = \max_{0 \le i \le q} \|y^{(i)}\|_B, \quad y \in X,$$

where $B = [a,b]$,

$$\|f\|_B = \max_{x \in B} |f(x)|, \quad f \in C(B), \tag{11.1}$$

and q is the order of the given differential equation. Further, we will always define $Y = C[a,b]$ and

$$\|r\|_Y = \|r\|_B, \quad r \in Y.$$

Throughout this section we choose X_n to be the $(n+1)$-dimensional (!) space of all polynomials of degree at most n, defined on the interval $[a,b]$, and set

$$E_n(f) = \inf\{\|f - p\|_B \mid p \in X_n\}$$

for $f \in C[a,b]$. We recall that $E_n(f)$ tends to zero for $n \to \infty$ by WEIERSTRASS' theorem, and that the rate of this convergence can be estimated by the theorems of JACKSON (cf. CHENEY [66]).

We will in particular utilize the results of Sect. 8 on discretization. For that let $\{B_k\}_{k \in \mathbb{N}}$ generally be a sequence of subsets of B which satisfies Assumption 8.1 and in addition (8.15). (We note that (8.15) is not needed in Sect. 11.1). Moreover, let B_k, $k \in \mathbb{N}$, contain at least $n+1$ pairwisely distinct points. Thus $\|r\|_{B_k} = 0$ implies $r = 0$ on B for $r \in X_n$ where

$$\|f\|_{B_k} = \max_{x \in B_k} |f(x)|, \quad f \in C(B). \tag{11.2}$$

Let us finally point out that we will rename here solutions $\hat{a}$, $\hat{a}_n$, $\hat{a}_n^k$, of (P), (P_n), and (P_n^k) by $\hat{y}$, $\hat{y}_n$, and $\hat{y}_n^k$, respectively.

Remark 11.1. The derivations of the stability inequalities of the type (6.1) for the problems below would allow us to equip $Y = C[a,b]$ with the L_1-norm

$$\|f\|_B = \int_a^b |f(x)|dx, \quad f \in C[a,b],$$

instead of the maximum norm (11.1). Further, due to Conclusion 8.1 (2), all results on the discretized problems below are also valid for $\|\cdot\|_{B_k}$ being the corresponding discrete L_1-semi norm.

11.1. LINEAR BOUNDARY VALUE PROBLEMS OF SECOND ORDER

Let a_0, a_1, $r \in C[a,b]$ and α_i, $\beta_i \in \mathbb{R}$, $0 \le i \le 2$, with $\alpha_0^2 + \alpha_1^2 \ne 0$ and $\beta_0^2 + \beta_1^2 \ne 0$ be given. Then with

$$N_a(y) = \alpha_0 y(a) + \alpha_1 y'(a),$$
$$N_b(y) = \beta_0 y(b) + \beta_1 y'(b),$$

and $X = C^2[a,b]$ we set here

$$A = A_k = \{y \in X \mid N_a(y) = \alpha_2,\ \ N_b(y) = \beta_2\},\quad k \in \mathbb{N}. \tag{11.3}$$

Furthermore, we define $T : X \to Y = C[a,b]$ by

$$Ty = y'' + a_1 y' + a_0 y.$$

Hence (P) becomes here the linear boundary value problem of second order

(P) For $r \in Y$ given find $y \in A$ such that $Ty = r$.

It is well-known that (P) possesses a unique solution $\hat{y} \in A$, provided that the following assumption is fulfilled (cf. WALTER [72], p. 175).

Assumption 11.1. The homogeneous boundary value problem $Ty = 0$, $N_a(y) = N_b(y) = 0$ has no nontrivial solution.

Thus, Assumption 11.1 ensures that our general Assumption A is fulfilled here. Concerning Assumption B, we next prove the following.

Lemma 11.1. $\bigcup_{n\geq 0} (X_n \cap A)$ is dense in A (11.3). For $n \geq 3$ we have moreover $X_n \cap A \neq \emptyset$ and

$$\min_{p\in(X_n\cap A)} \|y - p\|_X \leq C E_{n-2}(y''),\quad y \in A,$$

where

$$C = \max\{1,(b-a)^2\}[1 + 2\max\{\frac{4}{27}(b-a), 1, \frac{4}{b-a}, \frac{4}{(b-a)^2}\}]. \tag{11.4}$$

Proof. Let $y \in A$ be fixed and $p_{n-2} \in X_{n-2}$ be that polynomial for which $E_{n-2}(y'') = \|y'' - p_{n-2}\|_B$. Further, let $w_n \in X_n$ be the polynomial with

$$w_n''(x) = p_{n-2}(x),\quad w_n'(a) = y'(a),\quad w_n(a) = y(a). \tag{11.5}$$

Then by integration we can easily conclude that

$$\|y - w_n\|_X \leq C_1\, E_{n-2}(y'') \tag{11.6}$$

where $C_1 = \max\{1, (b-a)^2\}$. Next we define

$$s_n(x) = \frac{(x-a)^2(x-b)}{(b-a)^2} A_2 + \frac{(x-a)^2}{(b-a)^2}\left(1 - 2\,\frac{x-b}{b-a}\right) A_1$$

with

$$A_1 = y(b) - w_n(b), \quad A_2 = y'(b) - w_n'(b).$$

Since

$$s_n(a) = 0, \quad s_n'(a) = 0, \quad s_n(b) = A_1, \quad s_n'(b) = A_2,$$

and (11.5) holds true, we have that $w_n + s_n$ is in $X_n \cap A$ for $n \geq 3$. We can further compute

$$\begin{aligned} \|s_n\|_X &\leq \max\left\{\frac{4}{27}(b-a), 1, \frac{4}{b-a}\right\} |A_2| + \max\left\{1, \frac{1}{b-a}, \frac{4}{(b-a)^2}\right\} |A_1| \\ &\leq C_2 \|y - w_n\|_X \end{aligned}$$

where

$$C_2 = 2\max\left\{\frac{4}{27}(b-a), 1, \frac{4}{b-a}, \frac{4}{(b-a)^2}\right\}.$$

Consequently, employing (11.6), we arrive at

$$\begin{aligned} \min_{p\in(X_n\cap A)} \|y - p\|_X &\leq \|y - w_n - s_n\|_X \leq (1 + C_2) \|y - w_n\|_X \\ &\leq C_1(1 + C_2)E_{n-2}(y''). \end{aligned}$$ □

At this point we would like to remark that essentially all results of this subsection have been proved before by SCHMIDT and WIGGINS [79], however, with differing arguments. The proof of the following theorem is a straightforward application of the theory developed in Chapter 1, where we refer to (P), (P_n), and (P_n^k) with the specifications of this subsection.

Theorem 11.1. Let Assumption 11.1 be fulfilled and let $\hat{y} \in A$ be the unique solution of (P). Then for $n \geq 3$ we have:

(1) (P_n) and (P_n^k), $k \in \mathbb{N}$, possess solutions $\hat{y}_n \in (X_n \cap A)$ and $\hat{y}_n^k \in (X_n \cap A)$, respectively. If a_0 and a_1 are constant and $a_0 \neq 0$, $\hat{y}_n$ and $\hat{y}_n^k$ are unique.

(2) $\lim\limits_{n\to\infty} \rho_n = 0$.

(3) For n fixed, $\lim\limits_{k\to\infty} \rho_n^k = \rho_n$. In particular, for constant a_0 and a_1, $a_0 \neq 0$, also all assumptions of Theorem 8.1 (3) and (4) are satisfied.

(4) Let $K_1 = 1 + \|a_1\|_B + \|a_0\|_B$. There exists a constant K_2 (which is computable if a Green's function for the homogeneous problem $Ty = 0$, $N_a(y) = N_b(y) = 0$ is known) so that for $y \in A$

$$K_1^{-1}\|r - Ty\|_B \leq \|\hat{y} - y\|_X \leq K_2\|r - Ty\|_B.$$

(5) $\|\hat{y} - \hat{y}_n\|_X \leq K_1 K_2 CE_{n-2}(\hat{y}'')$ with C (11.4).

(6) $\lim\limits_{n\to\infty} \|\hat{y} - \hat{y}_n\|_X = 0$.

Proof. Obviously, T is Lipschitz continuous on X with constant $K_1 = 1 + \|a_1\|_B + \|a_0\|_B$. Further, $T^{-1} : Y \to A \subseteq X$ exists and is Lipschitz continuous on Y with constant K_2 which is computable if the Green's function of the homogeneous problem $Ty = 0$, $N_a(y) = N_b(y) = 0$ is known (cf. SCHMIDT/WIGGINS [79]) or else if $\max\{\|a_1\|_B, \|a_0\|_B\}$ is sufficiently small (cf. KRABS [79], p. 150).

Since $X_n \cap A$ is a linear variety in X_n, we can conclude the existence of $\hat{y}_n$ and $\hat{y}_n^k$ from Theorem 5.1 by equipping Y with the norms $\|\cdot\|_B$ and $\|\cdot\|_{B_k}$, respectively. If a_0, a_1 are constant and if $a_0 \neq 0$, Tx^n is a polynomial of degree n and hence $\{Tx^0,\dots,Tx^n\}$ satisfies 'Haar's condition' on B and B_k, which implies the uniqueness of $\hat{y}_n$ and $\hat{y}_n^k$ (see e.g. CHENEY [66]). (This last result was already given by YOUNG [07], however, with a different proof).

(2) follows by Theorem 3.1. Further, (3) can be concluded from Theorems 8.1 and 8.2, and (4) is a consequence of the Lipschitz continuity of T and T^{-1}.

For the proof of (5) we refer to Lemma 11.1 and Theorem 7.1, whereas finally (6) is an implication of (5). □

11.2. THE FIRST ORDER INITIAL VALUE PROBLEM

Let γ, a, and c with $c > a$ be real numbers. Further, for $\theta > 0$ arbitrarily small, determine $d > 0$ so that with

$$R = \{(x,y) \in \mathbb{R}^2 \mid \ a \leq x \leq c, \ \ \gamma - d - \theta \leq y \leq \gamma + d + \theta\} \tag{11.7}$$

f is a function that satisfies

Assumption 11.2. $f \in C(R)$ and there is a number $L > 0$ so that for all (x,y), $(x,\bar{y}) \in R$

$$|f(x,y) - f(x,\bar{y})| \leq L \ |y - \bar{y}|. \tag{11.8}$$

Further, let

$$M = \max_{(x,y)\in R} |f(x,y)|$$

and

$$b = \min(c , \frac{d}{M}) .$$

Then for $X = C^1[a,b]$ and $B = [a,b]$ we set

$$V = \{y \in X \mid \ y(a) = \gamma\} \tag{11.9}$$

and

$$A = \{y \in V \mid \ \gamma - d \leq y(x) \leq \gamma + d \ \text{ for all } x \in B\}. \tag{11.10}$$

Finally we define the operator $T : A \subseteq X \to Y = C[a,b]$ by

$$Ty = y' - f(\cdot,y)$$

such that (P) is here the first order initial value problem

(P) Find $y \in A$ such that $Ty = 0$.

Note that $r \in Y$ is the zero function here.

It is well-known that under Assumption 11.2 (P) possesses a unique solution $\hat{y} \in A$ (see WALTER [72], p. 51) so that Assumption A is fulfilled here. With reference to Assumption B, we next prove the following.

Lemma 11.2. $\bigcup_{n\geq 0}(X_n \cap A)$ is dense in A (11.10), where $X_n \cap A$ is nonempty for all $n \geq 0$. Provided that $n \geq 1$ is sufficiently large such that $E_{n-1}(y') \leq d/\max(1, b-a)$, we have in particular

$$\min_{p\in(X_n\cap A)} \|y - p\|_X \leq CE_{n-1}(y')$$

for each $y \in A$ where

$$C = \max(1, b-a)\{1 + \max(1, \frac{\|y'\|_B}{d})\}.$$

Proof. We note that the density of $\bigcup_{n\geq 0}(X_n \cap A)$ in A can be immediately concluded from Lemma 2.1 and that $y = \gamma$ is in $X_n \cap A$ for all $n \geq 0$.

For $y \in V$ let now $w_n \in X_n$ be such that $E_{n-1}(y') = \|y' - w_n'\|_B$ and $w_n(a) = y(a)$. Hence w_n is in $X_n \cap V$, and we can easily obtain by integration

$$\min_{p\in(X_n\cap V)} \|y - p\|_X \leq \|y - w_n\|_X \leq KE_{n-1}(y'), \quad y \in V, \tag{11.11}$$

where $K = \max(1, b-a)$.

We fix now $y \in A\setminus(X_n \cap A)$. $y_0(x) = \gamma$ is element of the interior $\mathring{A}$ of A relative to V. Hence also $v(x) = y(x) + \delta(y_0(x) - y(x))$ is in $\mathring{A}$ for every $\delta\in(0,1]$ due to the convexity of A. In particular, we choose $\delta = KE_{n-1}(y')/d$ where n shall be sufficiently large so that $\delta \leq 1$. Then defining $\hat{p}_n \in (X_n \cap V)$ by

$$\|v - \hat{p}_n\|_X = \min_{p\in(X_n\cap V)} \|v - p\|_X \tag{11.12}$$

and using the rule $E_{n-1}(\sigma y') = |\sigma|\, E_{n-1}(y')$ for $\sigma \in \mathbb{R}$ (cf. DAVIS [75], p. 329), we obtain from (11.11)

$$\|v - \hat{p}_n\|_X \leq K(1-\delta)E_{n-1}(y') \leq KE_{n-1}(y') = \delta d. \tag{11.13}$$

Since further

$$\gamma\delta + (1-\delta)(\gamma - d) \le v(x) \le \gamma\delta + (1-\delta)(\gamma + d)$$

for all $x \in B$, we can conclude from (11.13) that $\hat{p}_n$ is element of $X_n \cap A$. Therefore, we finally arrive at

$$\begin{aligned}\min_{p\in(X_n\cap A)} \|y-p\|_X &\le \|y-\hat{p}_n\|_X \le \|v-\hat{p}_n\|_X + \delta\, \|y_0 - y\|_X \\ &\le KE_{n-1}(y') + \delta \max(d, \|y'\|_B) \\ &\le K(1+\max(1, \frac{\|y'\|_B}{d}))E_{n-1}(y'). \quad \square \end{aligned} \tag{11.14}$$

In order to be able to apply the results of Sect. 8, we have further to verify Assumption 8.2 here. For its proof we will need the following somewhat surprising lemma, which is fundamental for our further investigations.

<u>Lemma 11.3.</u> Let $B \subset \mathbb{R}$ be compact and $\{B_k\}_{k\in\mathbb{N}}$ be a sequence of compact subsets of B which satisfies (8.15). Further, let $f_0, f_1, \ldots, f_n$ be functions which are r times continuously differentiable on B and let $f_1, \ldots, f_n$ be linearly independent on $B_{\bar{k}}$ for $\bar{k} = \bar{k}(n) \in \mathbb{N}$. Then if $\|\cdot\|_B$ and $\|\cdot\|_{B_k}$ are defined by (11.1) and (11.2) and if

$$S_\alpha^k = \{f \in f_0 + \langle f_1, \ldots, f_n\rangle \mid \|f\|_{B_k} \le \alpha\},$$

there exists a constant C_1 (depending on n) such that

$$\max_{0\le i\le r} \|f^{(i)}\|_B \le C_1 \quad \text{for all } f \in S_\alpha^k \text{ and all } k \ge \bar{k}.$$

<u>Proof.</u> Let $k \ge \bar{k}$ be fixed and $f = f_0 + \sum_{j=1}^{n} a_j f_j$, $a \in \mathbb{R}^n$, be element of S_α^k. Then we have $\min_{\|a\|_1=1} \|\sum_{j=1}^{n} a_j f_j\|_{B_k} = \varphi_k > 0$ so that

$$\varphi_k \|a\|_1 \le \|\sum_{j=1}^{n} a_j f_j\|_{B_k} \le \alpha + \|f_0\|_B := \tilde{\alpha}$$

and, therefore, $\|a\|_1 \le \tilde{\alpha}/\varphi_k$. Consequently, we have for all $f \in S_\alpha^k$

$$\max_{0\le i\le r} \|f^{(i)}\|_B \le \max_{0\le i\le r} \|f_0^{(i)}\|_B + \max_{0\le i\le r} \max_{\|a\|_1\le\tilde{\alpha}/\varphi_k} \|\sum_{j=1}^{n} a_j f_j^{(i)}\|_B := C_k.$$

Finally, if $\{B_k\}_{k\in\mathbb{N}}$ is a sequence of sets as being assumed, we have $\varphi_k \le \varphi_{k+1}$ and hence $C_k \le C_{\bar{k}}$ for all $k \ge \bar{k}$. □

Now setting

$$A_k = \{y \in V \mid \gamma - d \le y(x) \le \gamma + d \quad \text{for all } x \in B_k\}, \tag{11.15}$$

where V is given by (11.9), we can prove

<u>Lemma 11.4.</u> We fix $n \ge 0$. Then for A and A_k, $k \in \mathbb{N}$, defined by (11.10) and (11.15), Assumptions 8.2 (i) and (ii) are satisfied. Moreover, there exists a number $\hat{k} = \hat{k}(n,\theta) \in \mathbb{N}$ such that for $y \in (X_n \cap A_k)$, $k \ge \hat{k}$, and x, $\xi \in [a,b]$, $(x, y(\xi))$ is in R (11.7).

<u>Proof.</u> By virtue of our assumptions on $\{B_k\}_{k\in\mathbb{N}}$, $\{A_k\}_{k\in\mathbb{N}}$ satisfies Assumption 8.2 (i). Further, by Lemma 11.2 $X_n \cap A$ is nonempty for all $n \ge 0$. So let us verify now Assumption 8.2 (ii), i.e. that for $\varepsilon > 0$ there is a number $k_0 \in \mathbb{N}$ such that

$$\inf_{z\in(X_n\cap A)} \|z - y\|_X < \varepsilon \quad \text{for all } y \in (X_n \cap A_k),\ k \ge k_0. \tag{11.16}$$

For that we observe first that due to our general assumptions on $\{B_k\}_{k\in\mathbb{N}}$ there is a constant C_1 (depending on n) by Lemma 11.3 so that

$$\|y\|_X \le C_1 \quad \text{for all } y \in (X_n \cap A_k) \text{ and all } k \in \mathbb{N}. \tag{11.17}$$

Hence setting $\mu_k = C_1\, h(B_k, B)$ for $k \in \mathbb{N}$ fixed, we can get that if y is in $X_n \cap A_k$, for each $x \in B$ there is a $\xi \in B_k$ such that

$$|y(x) - y(\xi)| \le \mu_k$$

by the mean value theorem. Therefore, defining

$$M_k = \{y \in (X_n \cap V) \mid \gamma - d - \mu_k \le y(x) \le \gamma + d + \mu_k \quad \text{for all } x \in B\}, \qquad (11.18)$$

we note that $(X_n \cap A) \subseteq (X_n \cap A_k) \subseteq M_k$ for all $k \in \mathbb{N}$.

Let now $y_0(x) = \gamma$. Then for all $y \in M_k$, $y_0 + \lambda_k(y-y_0)$ with $\lambda_k = d/(d+\mu_k)$ lies in $X_n \cap A$. Consequently, we have for all $y \in (X_n \cap A_k)$, $k \in \mathbb{N}$ fixed,

$$\inf_{z \in (X_n \cap A)} \|z - y\|_X \le \|y_0 + \lambda_k(y-y_0) - y\|_X$$

$$= (1 - \lambda_k)\ \|y_0 - y\|_X \le \frac{\mu_k}{d + \mu_k} (\|y_0\|_X + C_1)$$

where (11.17) was used. Due to our assumptions on $\{B_k\}_{k \in \mathbb{N}}$, μ_k tends monotonically decreasing to zero for $k \to \infty$ so that (11.16) is proved.

Finally we choose $\hat{k} = \hat{k}(n,\theta)$ sufficiently large such that $\mu_k \le \theta$ for all $k \ge \hat{k}$. Then for all $y \in (X_n \cap A_k)$, $k \ge \hat{k}$, we have $\gamma - d - \theta \le y(\xi) \le \gamma + d + \theta$ for all $\xi \in [a,b]$ so that the proof is complete. □

By Lemma 11.4, (P_n^k) is well defined for all $n \ge 0$ and $k \ge \hat{k}(n,\theta)$.

We are now in the position to prove the main result of this subsection.

<u>Theorem 11.2.</u> Let Assumption 11.2 be fulfilled so that $\hat{y} \in A$ is the unique solution of (P). Then we have:

(1) For $n \ge 0$ (P_n) and (P_n^k), $k \ge \hat{k}$, possess solutions $\hat{y}_n \in X_n \cap A$ and $\hat{y}_n^k \in (X_n \cap A_k)$, respectively, where $\hat{k} = \hat{k}(n,\theta)$ is determined by Lemma 11.4.

(2) $\lim_{n \to \infty} \rho_n = 0$.

(3) For $n \ge 0$ fixed, statements (1) - (3) of Theorem 8.1 hold here. In particular, $\lim_{k \to \infty} \rho_n^k = \rho_n$.

(4) For every $y \in A$

$$K_1^{-1}\ \|Ty\|_B \le \|\hat{y} - y\|_X \le K_2\ \|Ty\|_B$$

with $K_1 = 1 + L$ and $K_2 = \max(N, LN + 1)$ where

$$N = (b-a)\exp\{L(b-a)\}. \qquad (11.19)$$

(5) If $n \geq 1$ is sufficiently large so that $E_{n-1}(\hat{y}') \leq d/\max(1, b-a)$, we have

$$\|\hat{y} - \hat{y}_n\|_X \leq K_1 \; K_2 \; CE_{n-1}(\hat{y}')$$

where

$$C = \max(1, \; b-a)\{1 + \max(1, \; \frac{M}{d})\}.$$

(6) $\lim_{n\to\infty} \|\hat{y} - \hat{y}_n\|_X = 0.$

Proof. It is easy to show that T is Lipschitz continuous on A with constant $K_1 = 1 + L$. Let us next compute a stability constant K_2.

For $y \in A$ we obtain by integration

$$y(x) = \gamma + \int_a^x [f(\xi,y(\xi)) + (Ty)(\xi)]d\xi, \quad x\in[a,b],$$

so that employing (11.8) we get for $y, \; z \in A$ and $x \in [a,b]$

$$|y(x) - z(x)| \leq (b-a) \; \|Ty - Tz\|_B + L \int_a^x |y(\xi) - z(\xi)| \; d\xi.$$

Application of Gronwall's lemma (see WALTER [72], p. 214) yields further for $x\in[a,b]$

$$|y(x) - z(x)| \leq (b-a) \; \|Ty - Tz\|_B \; \exp\{L(x-a)\}. \tag{11.20}$$

Moreover, for all $x \in [a,b]$ we can derive

$$\begin{aligned} |y'(x) - z'(x)| &\leq |f(x,y(x)) - f(x,z(x))| + |(Ty)(x) - (Tz)(x)| \\ &\leq L|y(x) - z(x)| + \|Ty - Tz\|_B \\ &\leq [L(b-a)\exp\{L(x-a)\} + 1] \; \|Ty - Tz\|_B. \end{aligned} \tag{11.21}$$

Combining (11.20) and (11.21), we finally arrive at

$$\|y - z\|_X \leq \max(N, \; LN + 1) \; \|Ty - Tz\|_B$$

with N defined by (11.19). Thereby (4) has been proved.

By Lemma 11.4, T is continuous on $X_n \cap A_{\hat{k}}$. Further, if y is in $C_\alpha^{\hat{k}}(X_n \cap A_{\hat{k}})$ for $\alpha > 0$, y is in $X_n \cap A_{\hat{k}}$ such that $\|y\|_{B_{\hat{k}}} \le |\gamma| + d$. So using Lemma 11.3 we can infer that there exists a constant C_1 independent of y such that $\|y\|_X \le C_1$. Consequently, $C_\alpha^{\hat{k}}(X_n \cap A_{\hat{k}})$ is bounded in X. Hence application of Lemma 8.2 proofs statement (1). (We note here that for the existence of $\hat{y}_n$ we could refer to Conclusion 5.1 as well).

(2) follows directly from Theorem 3.1. So let us verify (3) now.

We showed above that the assumptions of Lemma 8.2 are fulfilled here. Hence, in order to apply Theorem 8.1, we only need to prove the equicontinuity of $\{T\hat{y}_n^k\}_{k \ge \hat{k}}$ on B. For that we note first that by Lemma 11.3 and because of (8.15) there exists a constant C_2 such that

$$\max_{0 \le i \le 2} \|y^{(i)}\|_B \le C_2 \quad \text{for all } y \in (X_n \cap A_k), \quad k \ge \hat{k},$$

(cf. the prove of (1) above). Next we select $\varepsilon > 0$ such that $|f(x,y) - f(\bar{x},\bar{y})| < \varepsilon$ for all (x,y), $(\bar{x},\bar{y}) \in R$ with $\max\{|x-\bar{x}|, |y-\bar{y}|\} < \delta$. Then recalling that due to Lemma 11.4 $(x, \hat{y}_n^k(\xi))$ is in R for all x, $\xi \in [a,b]$ and $k \ge \hat{k}$, we obtain for all x, $\xi \in [a,b]$ with $|x-\xi| < \delta$ and $k \ge \hat{k}$

$$\begin{aligned}
|(T\hat{y}_n^k)(x) - (T\hat{y}_n^k)(\xi)| &\le |\hat{y}_n^{k'}(x) - \hat{y}_n^{k'}(\xi)| + |f(x,\hat{y}_n^k(x)) - f(\xi,\hat{y}_n^k(\xi))| \\
&\le C_2|x-\xi| + |f(x,\hat{y}_n^k(x)) - f(x,\hat{y}_n^k(\xi))| + |f(x,\hat{y}_n^k(\xi)) - f(\xi,\hat{y}_n^k(\xi))| \\
&\le C_2\,\delta + L\,C_2\,\delta + \varepsilon.
\end{aligned}$$

(5) follows from Theorem 7.1 in connection with Lemma 11.2 where $\|\hat{y}'\|_B = \|f(\cdot,\hat{y})\|_B \le M$ is used. Finally, (6) is a consequence of (5). □

If f satisfies a Lipschitz condition for all $(x,y) \in [a,c] \times \mathbb{R}$, (P) possesses a unique solution $\hat{y} \in C^1[a,c]$. Setting $y = \hat{y}$ and $z = \gamma$ in (11.20), we can obtain in this case

$$\|\hat{y} - z\|_B \le (b-a)\, \|f(\cdot,z)\|_B \exp\{L(b-a)\} := \eta.$$

Hence, in order to maintain the definitions of A and A_k with finite bounds on y, we can define $d = \eta$ there. (Then $\hat{k} = 1$ in Theorem 11.2 (1)). Otherwise, we would have $d = \infty$ and hence $V = A = A_k$ for all $k \in \mathbb{N}$, which on a first view seems to be more reasonable with regard to computations. However, in that case, boundedness of $C_\alpha^k(X_n \cap A_k)$ and, therefore, the existence of $\hat{y}_n^k$ and the convergence of ρ_n^k to ρ_n for $k \to \infty$ cannot be guaranteed any more without additional assumptions on f. Examples of such assumptions are given by the following two lemmas.

<u>Lemma 11.5.</u> Let f satisfy Assumption 11.2 with $R = [a,c] \times \mathbb{R}$, so that the domain of T can be extended to all of X, and let

$$A = A_k = V = \{y \in X \mid \ y(a) = \gamma\}, \quad k \in \mathbb{N}. \tag{11.22}$$

Further, let f have the following properties.

(i) There is a number $r \in \mathbb{R}$ so that $f(x,\lambda y) = \lambda^r f(x,y)$ for each $\lambda \in \mathbb{R} \setminus \{0\}$. If $r = 1$, let in addition $\|Tz\|_{B_k} \neq 0$ for all $z \in X_n$.

(ii) $\|f(\cdot,y)\|_{B_k} = 0$ for $y \in X_n$ implies $y = 0$ on B.

Then $C_\alpha^k(X_n \cap A)$ is bounded for each $\alpha > 0$ and $k \in \mathbb{N}$.

<u>Proof.</u> Let Z_n be the space generated by the n linearly independent functions $v_i(x) = x^i - a^i$, $i = 1,\dots,n$. Then for each $y \in (X_n \cap A)$ there is a $z_y \in Z_n$ such that $y(x) = \gamma + z_y(x)$. Further, for each $y \in C_\alpha^k(X_n \cap A)$ we have

$$\|Tz_y\|_{B_k} \leq \|Ty\|_{B_k} + \|T(y-\gamma) - Ty\|_{B_k} \leq \alpha + L|\gamma| := \bar{\alpha}.$$

Hence it is sufficient to prove the boundedness of $C_{\bar{\alpha}}^k(Z_n)$ in order to prove the boundedness of $C_\alpha^k(X_n \cap A)$. For that let $z(x) = \sum_{i=1}^{n} e_i v_i(x)$ with $\|e\|_1 \neq 0$ be element of Z_n and

$$K = \{e \in \mathbb{R}^n \mid \ \|e\|_1 = 1\}.$$

Let now first $r = 1$. Then, due to property (i) of f, we have

$$\sigma = \min_{e \in K} \|\sum_{i=1}^{n} e_i v_i' - f(\cdot, \sum_{i=1}^{n} e_i v_i)\|_{B_k} > 0$$

so that for all $z \in C_{\bar{\alpha}}^k(Z_n)$

$$\bar{\alpha} \geq \|Tz\|_{B_k} = \|e\|_1 \, \| \sum_{i=1}^{n} \frac{e_i}{\|e\|_1} v_i' - f(\cdot, \sum_{i=1}^{n} \frac{e_i}{\|e\|_1} v_i) \|_{B_k} \geq \|e\|_1 \, \sigma.$$

Next we define

$$\mu = \max_{e \in K} \|f(\cdot, \sum_{i=1}^{n} e_i v_i)\|_{B_k}$$

and

$$\upsilon = \min_{e \in K} \| \sum_{i=1}^{n} e_i v_i' \|_{B_k} . \tag{11.23}$$

Due to our assumptions on f and B_k, we have $\mu > 0$ and $\upsilon > 0$. Hence, if $r < 1$, we obtain for all $z \in C_{\bar{\alpha}}^{k}(Z_n)$

$$\| \sum_{i=1}^{n} e_i v_i' \|_{B_k} \leq \bar{\alpha} + \|f(\cdot, \sum_{i=1}^{n} e_i v_i)\|_{B_k}$$

so that

$$\|e\|_1 \upsilon \leq \bar{\alpha} + \mu \, \|e\|_1^r$$

which only can hold true if $\|e\|_1$ is sufficiently small.

Finally, we consider the case $r > 1$. Setting

$$\eta = \min_{e \in K} \|f(\cdot, \sum_{i=1}^{n} e_i v_i)\|_{B_k}$$

and observing that η is positive, we deduce for $z \in C_{\bar{\alpha}}^{k}(Z_n)$

$$\|f(\cdot, \sum_{i=1}^{n} e_i v_i)\|_{B_k} \leq \bar{\alpha} + \| \sum_{i=1}^{n} e_i v_i' \|_{B_k}$$

and, therefore,

$$\eta \|e\|_1^r \leq \bar{\alpha} + \|e\|_1 \max_{1 \leq i \leq n} \|v_i'\|_{B_k} ,$$

which again can only be true for $\|e\|_1$ being sufficiently small. So in each case $\|e\|_1$ and consequently $C_{\bar{\alpha}}^{k}(Z_n)$ is bounded. □

Lemma 11.6. Let f satisfy Assumption 11.2 with $R = [a,c] \times \mathbb{R}$ and let the domain of T be extended to X. Further, let A be defined by (11.22). If there exists a constant K such that

$$\|f(\cdot,y)\|_B \le K \quad \text{for all } y \in X_n,$$

then $C_\alpha^k(X_n \cap A)$ is bounded for each $\alpha > 0$ and $k \in \mathbb{N}$.

Proof. According to the previous proof, it is sufficient to verify the boundedness of $C_{\underline{\alpha}}^{\underline{k}}(Z_n)$. If again $z(x) = \sum_{i=1}^{n} e_i v_i(x)$ is element of Z_n, we have for $z \in C_{\underline{\alpha}}^{\underline{k}}(Z_n)$

$$\Big\| \sum_{i=1}^{n} e_i v_i' \Big\|_{B_k} \le \bar{\alpha} + \Big\| f(\cdot, \sum_{i=1}^{n} e_i v_i) \Big\|_{B_k}.$$

Hence, with υ (11.23) we obtain

$$\|e\|_1 \upsilon \le \bar{\alpha} + \Big\| f(\cdot, \sum_{i=1}^{n} e_i v_i) \Big\|_{B_k} \le \bar{\alpha} + K. \qquad \square$$

11.3. A SECOND ORDER BOUNDARY VALUE PROBLEM

Let a, b, c, d, e and f be real numbers with $b > a$, $d > c$, and $f > e$. Moreover, let γ_1 and γ_2 be elements of the open interval (c,d) and $(\gamma_2 - \gamma_1)/(b-a) \in (e,f)$. Finally let σ and τ be arbitrarily small real numbers and

$$D = \{(x,y,z) \in \mathbb{R}^3 \mid \; a \le x \le b, \;\; c - \sigma \le y \le d + \sigma, \;\; e - \tau \le z \le f + \tau\}. \tag{11.24}$$

Then g shall be a function which fulfills

Assumption 11.3. $g \in C(D)$ and there are numbers $L_1 > 0$, $L_2 > 0$ so that for all (x,y,z), $(x,\bar{y},\bar{z}) \in D$

$$|g(x,y,z) - g(x,\bar{y},\bar{z})| \le L_1 |y - \bar{y}| + L_2 |z - \bar{z}|$$

where

$$\tilde{C} := L_1 \frac{(b-a)^2}{8} + L_2 \frac{b-a}{2} < 1. \tag{11.25}$$

Next we set here $X = C^2[a,b]$,

$$V = \{y \in X | \ \ y(a) = \gamma_1, \ \ y(b) = \gamma_2\}, \tag{11.26}$$

and

$$A = \{y \in V | \ \ c \leq y(x) \leq d, \ e \leq y'(x) \leq f \ \ \text{for all } x \in B\} \tag{11.27}$$

where $B = [a,b]$. Then with $T : A \subseteq X \to Y = C[a,b]$ defined by

$$Ty = y'' + g(\cdot,y,y'), \tag{11.28}$$

(P) becomes here the second order boundary value problem

$$\text{(P)} \quad \text{Find } y \in A \text{ such that } Ty = 0. \tag{11.29}$$

Sufficient conditions for the unique solvability of (P), i.e. for Assumption A to be satisfied here, are, for instance, derived by BERNFELD and LAKSHMIKANTHAM [74]. In particular, Assumption A is fulfilled for $D = [a,b] \times \mathbb{R} \times \mathbb{R}$.

With regard to Assumption B, we now prove the following.

<u>Lemma 11.7.</u> $\bigcup_{n \geq 0} (X_n \cap A)$ is dense in A (11.27) where $X_n \cap A$ is nonempty for $n \geq 1$. In particular, if $n \geq 2$ is sufficiently large so that $E_{n-2}(y'') \leq \zeta/C_0$ with

$$\zeta = \min\{\min(\gamma_1,\gamma_2) - c, \ d - \max(\gamma_1,\gamma_2), \ \frac{\gamma_2-\gamma_1}{b-a} - e, \ f - \frac{\gamma_2-\gamma_1}{b-a}\} \tag{11.30}$$

and

$$C_0 = \max\{1, (b-a)^2\}[1 + \max(1, \frac{1}{b-a})], \tag{11.31}$$

we have

$$\min_{p \in (X_n \cap A)} \|y - p\|_X \leq C \, E_{n-2}(y'')$$

for each $y \in A$ and

$$C = C_0\{1 + \zeta^{-1} \max(d-c, \ f-e, \ \|y''\|_B)\}. \tag{11.32}$$

Proof. For $y \in V$ (11.26), let $w_n \in X_n$, $n \geq 2$, be the polynomial such that $E_{n-2}(y'') = \|y'' - w_n''\|_B$, $w_n'(a) = y'(a)$, and $w_n(a) = y(a)$ holds true. Defining here

$$s_n(x) = \frac{x-a}{b-a}(y(b) - w_n(b))$$

and following the proof of Lemma 11.1, we can deduce

$$\min_{p \in (X_n \cap V)} \|y - p\|_X \leq C_0 \, E_{n-2}(y''), \quad y \in V,$$

with C_0 (11.31).

We proceed now as in the proof of Lemma 11.2. Due to our assumptions

$$y_0(x) = \frac{\gamma_1(b-x) + \gamma_2(x-a)}{b-a} \in X_n, \quad n \geq 1, \tag{11.33}$$

is in the interior $\mathring{A}$ of A relative to V. Hence for $y \in A \setminus (X_n \cap A)$ and $\delta = C_0 \, E_{n-2}(y'')/\zeta \leq 1$ with ζ (11.30), also $v(x) = y(x) + \delta(y_0(x) - y(x))$ is in $\mathring{A}$. Moreover, if $\hat{p}_n$ is given by (11.12) for V (11.26), we obtain in analogy to (11.13)

$$\|v - \hat{p}_n\|_X \leq \delta\zeta.$$

Since for all $x \in [a,b]$ we have

$$c < \min(\gamma_1, \gamma_2) \leq y_0(x) \leq \max(\gamma_1, \gamma_2) < d$$

and

$$e < y_0'(x) = \frac{\gamma_2 - \gamma_1}{b-a} < f,$$

we can further easily check that $\hat{p}_n$ is element of A. So using

$$\|y_0 - y\|_X \leq \max(d-c,\ f-e,\ \|y''\|_B), \quad y \in A,$$

we finally attain similarly to (11.14)

$$\min_{p \in (X_n \cap A)} \|y - p\|_X \leq C \, E_{n-2}(y'')$$

with C (11.32). □

For V (11.26) let now

$$A_k = \{y \in V \mid \; c \le y(x) \le d, \;\; e \le y'(x) \le f \;\; \text{for all } x \in B_k\}. \qquad (11.34)$$

Then the proof of the following lemma can be carried out as the proof of Lemma 11.4.

Lemma 11.8. Let $n \ge 1$. Then for A (11.27) and A_k (11.34), $k \in \mathbb{N}$, Assumptions 8.2 (i) and (ii) are fulfilled. Furthermore, there exists a number $\tilde{k} = \tilde{k}(n,\sigma,\tau) \in \mathbb{N}$ such that for $y \in (X_n \cap A_k)$, $k \ge \tilde{k}$, and $x, \eta, \xi \in [a,b]$, $(x, y(\eta), y'(\xi))$ is in D (11.24).

Lemma 11.8 ensures that (P_n^k) is well defined for $n \ge 1$ and $k \ge \tilde{k}(n,\sigma,\tau)$. Thus we can now give the following theorem.

Theorem 11.3. Let Assumption 11.3 be fulfilled and let (P) (11.29) have a unique solution $\hat{y} \in A$. Then we have:

(1) For $n \ge 1$ (P_n) and (P_n^k), $k \ge \tilde{k}$, possess solutions $\hat{y}_n \in (X_n \cap A)$ and $\hat{y}_n^k \in (X_n \cap A_k)$, respectively, where $\tilde{k} = \tilde{k}(n,\sigma,\tau)$ is determined through Lemma 11.8.

(2) $\lim\limits_{n\to\infty} \rho_n = 0$.

(3) For $n \ge 1$ fixed, statements (1) - (3) of Theorem 8.1 are valid here. In particular, $\lim\limits_{k\to\infty} \rho_n^k = \rho_n$.

(4) For every $y \in A$ we have

$$K_1^{-1} \, \|Ty\|_B \le \|\hat{y}-y\|_X \le K_2 \, \|Ty\|_B$$

where

$$K_1 = 1 + L_1 + L_2, \quad K_2 = \frac{1}{1-\tilde{C}} \max\left\{\frac{(b-a)^2}{8}, \; \frac{b-a}{2}, \; 1\right\}$$

and $\tilde{C}$ is defined by (11.25).

(5) If $n \ge 2$ is sufficiently large so that $E_{n-2}(\hat{y}'') \le \zeta / C_0$ with ζ (11.30) and C_0 (11.31), we have

$$\|\hat{y} - \hat{y}_n\|_X \le K_1 K_2 C E_{n-2}(\hat{y}'')$$

where

$$C = C_0\{1 + \zeta^{-1} \max(d-c,\ f-e,\ \max_{(x,y,z)\in D} |g(x,y,z)|\}.$$

(6) $\lim_{n\to\infty} \|\hat{y} - \hat{y}_n\|_X = 0.$

<u>Proof.</u> Obviously, T is Lipschitz continuous on A with constant $K_1 = 1 + L_1 + L_2$. In order to derive a stability constant K_2, we modify here ideas of KRABS [79], p. 150. For that let $y \in A$ and

$$\beta_1 = \frac{1}{8}(b-a)^2, \quad \beta_2 = \frac{1}{2}(b-a).$$

Writing elements of A which satisfy (11.28) as integral equations by using the corresponding Green's function, we can obtain after some elementary manipulations (cf. KRABS [79])

$$\|\hat{y} - y\|_B \le \beta_1 \|Ty\|_B + \beta_1 L_1 \|\hat{y} - y\|_B + \beta_1 L_2 \|\hat{y}' - y'\|_B, \tag{11.35}$$

$$\|\hat{y}' - y'\|_B \le \beta_2 \|Ty\|_B + \beta_2 L_1 \|\hat{y} - y\|_B + \beta_2 L_2 \|\hat{y}' - y'\|_B, \tag{11.36}$$

$$\|\hat{y}'' - y''\|_B \le \|Ty\|_B + L_1 \|\hat{y} - y\|_B + L_2 \|\hat{y}' - y'\|_B. \tag{11.37}$$

Because of (11.25), the inequalities (11.35) and (11.36) yield further

$$\|\hat{y} - y\|_B \le \frac{\beta_1}{1 - \beta_1 L_1} \|Ty\|_B + \frac{\beta_1 L_2}{1 - \beta_1 L_1} \|\hat{y}' - y'\|_B, \tag{11.38}$$

$$\|\hat{y}' - y'\|_B \le \frac{\beta_2}{1 - \beta_2 L_2} \|Ty\|_B + \frac{\beta_2 L_1}{1 - \beta_2 L_2} \|\hat{y} - y\|_B. \tag{11.39}$$

Now inserting (11.39) into (11.38) and correspondingly (11.38) into (11.39) and noting that by (11.25)

$$\frac{\beta_1 \beta_2 L_1 L_2}{(1-\beta_1 L_1)(1-\beta_2 L_2)} < 1,$$

we can arrive at

$$\|\hat{y} - y\|_B \le \frac{\beta_1}{1 - \tilde{C}} \|Ty\|_B, \tag{11.40}$$

$$\|\hat{y}' - y'\|_B \le \frac{\beta_1}{1 - \tilde{C}} \|Ty\|_B, \tag{11.41}$$

where $\tilde{C}$ is defined by (11.25). Finally we get from (11.37) by employing (11.40) and (11.41)

$$\|\hat{y}'' - y''\|_B \le \frac{1}{1-\tilde{C}} \|Ty\|_B.$$

Hence (4) is verified. All other statements can be proved like the corresponding statements of Theorem 11.2 where we make here use of Lemmas 11.7 and 11.8. □

We would like to point out that the remarks following Theorem 11.2 can be transferred to the problem under consideration. So if g satisfies Assumption 11.3 on $D = [a,b] \times \mathbb{R} \times \mathbb{R}$ (which guarantees the unique solvability of (P)), for numerical purposes we either have to compute bounds c, d and e, f for $\hat{y}$ and $\hat{y}'$ by using (11.40), (11.41), and (11.33), or we set $A = A_k = V$ with V (11.26) and then have to guarantee the boundedness of the level sets $C_\alpha^k(X_n \cap A)$ by additional assumptions on g.

12. A WELL-POSED PROBLEM FOR THE HEAT EQUATION: A STEFAN PROBLEM

The direct application of the method of minimizing the defects to boundary value problems of partial differential equations normally requires the minimization of the defects in the differential equation(s) and in the boundary conditions (→ the 'mixed method'). Usually this general approach is numerically too expensive and, therefore, not advisable. However, in many situations one can simplify the minimization problem by choosing a complete family of functions which either satisfies the differential equation(s) (→ the 'boundary method') or the boundary conditions (→ the 'interior method'). Among these approaches the 'boundary method' is the most attractive and henceforth the most frequently used method since it often can be justified in a natural way by a maximum principle and since it usually requires the least numerical effort. However, it has to be remarked that complete families of solutions have only been found for relatively simple differential equations. (For examples of such families we refer to COLTON [80]).

To our knowledge COLLATZ [59] was the first who applied the 'boundary method' to the solution of boundary value problems (see also COLLATZ/KRABS [73], KRABS [79], and COLLATZ [80]). Later on COLLATZ' idea has been used by several other authors. In general these authors motivated their proceeding by a maximum principle but did not present any further numerical analysis. In this connection we refer to the survey articles by RABINOWITZ [68] and CHEUNG [78]. (In addition, CHEUNG [78] provides some elementary convergence analysis for linear problems). Let us also mention that the efficiency of the boundary method has been studied by COLLATZ, GÜNTHER and SPREKELS [76].

As far as we know, in case of partial differential equations defect minimization in its original form has only been tried for the solution of linear problems. (In this connection see e.g. WENDLAND [79] for a detailed presentation of an example, CHEUNG [78] for a survey, and GROTHKOPF [81] for a discussion of some numerical aspects in case of nonlinear problems). It is not difficult to derive a convergence analysis for most of these linear problems if one makes use of the arguments employed in this and the previous sections. Therefore, we turn here now directly to the solution of a nonlinear problem, a so-called Stefan problem. Our results will show that the method of defect minimization can also be successfully applied to the numerical solution of free boundary problems. For such problems this method has the particular advantage that it does not need any discretization of the interior of the underlying domain. The determination of the domain is part of a free boundary value problem itself and, therefore, a major difficulty in the construction of numerical methods for its solution.

<u>Assumption 12.1.</u> $\mathcal{T} > 0$ and $b \geq 0$ are given reals. Further, $c \in C[0,\mathcal{T}]$ with $c \leq 0$ in $[0,\mathcal{T}]$ and (if $b > 0$) $f \in C^2[0,b]$ with $f \geq 0$ in $[0,b]$, $f'(0) = c(0)$, and $f(b) = 0$ are well defined functions. In particular, we have $c(0) < 0$ in case $b = 0$.

Then we consider the following classical one-dimensional single-phase Stefan problem: find $(u,s) \in C^{2,1}(D_{\mathcal{T}}(s)) \cap C^{1,0}(\overline{D_{\mathcal{T}}(s)}) \times C^1[0,\mathcal{T}]$ such that

$$Lu(x,t) := u_{xx}(x,t) - u_t(x,t) = 0 \quad \text{in } D_T(s), \tag{12.1}$$

$$u_x(0,t) = c(t), \qquad 0 \le t \le T, \tag{12.2}$$

$$u(x,0) = f(x), \qquad 0 \le x \le b, \tag{12.3}$$

$$u(s(t),t) = 0, \qquad 0 \le t \le T, \tag{12.4}$$

$$u_x(s(t),t) = -\dot{s}(t), \qquad 0 \le t \le T, \tag{12.5}$$

$$s(0) = b, \tag{12.6}$$

where for $s \in C[0,T]$

$$D_T(s) = \{(x,t) \in \mathbb{R}^2 \mid \; 0 < x < s(t), \; 0 < t \le T\}.$$

(12.3) and all terms related to (12.3) in the following have to be omitted if $b = 0$.

It is well-known that under Assumption 12.1 problem (12.1-6) possesses a unique solution $(\hat{u},\hat{s}) \in C^{2,1}(D_T(\hat{s})) \cap C^{1,0}(\overline{D_T(\hat{s})}) \times C^1[0,T]$ which depends continuously on the data. Furthermore, $(\hat{u},\hat{s})$ satisfies the following inequalities

$$0 \le \hat{u}(x,t) \le H(t)(\hat{s}(t) - x) \quad \text{in } \overline{D_T(\hat{s})}, \tag{12.7}$$

$$0 \le \dot{\hat{s}}(t) \le H(t), \qquad 0 \le t \le T, \tag{12.8}$$

where with

$$\|g\|_t = \max_{0 \le \tau \le t} |g(\tau)|, \quad g \in C[0,t],$$

H is defined by

$$H(t) = \max\{\|c\|_t, \|f'\|_b\} \tag{12.9}$$

(see CANNON/PRIMICERIO [71] and FRIEDMAN [59,60], and note that GEVREY [13] proved continuity of u_x in $(b,0)$ for $b > 0$ in case $f \in C^2[0,b]$).

We now intend to apply the theory of Chapter 1 to problem (12.1-6). Unfortunately, this problem cannot be brought into the form of our model problem (P) because its solution space depends on the parameter s which itself is part of the solution. So we cannot apply our theory here directly, but we can proceed in a similar fashion as before.

Let Assumption 12.1 be fulfilled and $(\hat{u},\hat{s}) \in C^{2,1}(D_T(\hat{s})) \cap C^{1,0}(\overline{D_T(\hat{s})}) \times C^1[0,T]$ be the unique solution of (12.1-6). Then we define $(X, \|\cdot\|_X)$ to be the normed space which is determined by

$$X = \{u \in C^{2,1}(D_T(\hat{s})) \cap C^{1,0}(\overline{D_T(\hat{s})}) \cap C^{0,1}(\bar{\hat{s}}) \mid \; Lu = 0 \text{ in } D_T(\hat{s})\}$$

and

$$\|u\|_X = \max\{\|u\|_{\overline{D_T(\hat{s})}}, \quad \|u_x\|_{\overline{D_T(\hat{s})}}, \quad \|u_t(\hat{s}(\cdot),\cdot)\|_T\},$$

where $\|\cdot\|_{\overline{D_T(\hat{s})}}$ denotes the usual sup-norm on $\overline{D_T(\hat{s})}$, and we set

$$A^{(1)}(G) = \{u \in C(G) \mid u(b,0) = 0\}$$

for any set $G \subseteq \mathbb{R}^2$ containing the point $(b,0)$. Further, we choose $Z = C^1[0,T]$ and equip Z with the norm

$$\|s\|_Z = \max\{\|s\|_T, \quad \|\dot{s}\|_T\}, \quad s \in Z.$$

Finally, if

$$d = \begin{cases} -\,c(0) & \text{for } b = 0, \\ -\,f'(b) & \text{for } b > 0, \end{cases}$$

where Assumption 12.1 implies $d > 0$ for $b = 0$ and $d \geq 0$ for $b > 0$, and if C is any constant with

$$C > b + H(T)T, \tag{12.10}$$

we define

$$V = \{s \in Z \mid s(0) = b, \quad \dot{s}(0) = d\} \tag{12.11}$$

and

$$A^{(2)} = \{s \in V \mid 0 \leq s(t) \leq C \quad \text{for all } t \in [0,T]\}. \tag{12.12}$$

Hence, recalling (12.7) and (12.8), we can conclude that $(\hat{u},\hat{s})$ is element of $(X \cap A_1(\overline{D_T(\hat{s})}) \times (Z \cap A^{(2)})$. (Note that for $\hat{s} \in Z$, $\hat{u}_t(\hat{s}(\cdot),\cdot) \in C[0,T]$ follows from (12.4) and (12.5)).

We next select families of functions for the approximation of $\hat{u}$ and $\hat{s}$. In particular, we define $X_n(G) = \langle v_0, v_1, \ldots, v_n \rangle$ to be the space which is generated by the heat polynomials

$$v_i(x,t) = \sum_{k=0}^{[i/2]} \frac{i!}{(i-2k)!\,k!} x^{i-2k} t^k, \tag{12.13}$$

$0 \leq i \leq n$, given on $G \subseteq \mathbb{R}^2$ (cf. WIDDER [75]). Then observing that $X_n(\overline{D_T(\hat{s})})$ associated with the $\|\cdot\|_X$-norm is a subspace of X, we can make the following remark with regard to the completeness of the heat polynomials in X. (Note that density of $\bigcup_{n\geq 0} X_n(\overline{D_T(\hat{s})})$ in X readily implies density of $\bigcup_{n\geq 0} (X_n(\overline{D_T(\hat{s})}) \cap A^{(1)}(\overline{D_T(\hat{s})})$ in $X \cap A^{(1)}(\overline{D_T(\hat{s})})$.

<u>Remark 12.1.</u> By COLTON [80] the heat polynomials $\{v_i\}_{i\geq 0}$ are complete in $\{u \in C(\overline{D_T(s)}) \mid Lu = 0 \text{ in } D_T(s)\}$ if s is a positive analytic function. It is a conjecture that already nonnegativity and continuity of s are sufficient for such a result. (We note that by the results of RUBINSTEIN, FASANO, and PRIMICERIO [80] Stefan problems with a free boundary which is analytic in $[0,T]$ form a very poor class). Further, completeness of $\{v_i\}_{i\geq 0}$ in X can be expected, but has also not been shown yet.

Let now Z_m be the space of all polynomials on $[0,T]$ with degree at most m. Then the following holds true.

<u>Lemma 12.1.</u> $\bigcup_{m\geq 0} (Z_m \cap A^{(2)})$ is dense in $A^{(2)}$ (12.12). Further, $Z_m \cap A^{(2)}$ is nonempty for all $m \in \mathbb{N}$.

<u>Proof.</u> V (12.11) is a linear variety in Z. Furthermore, it is well-known that $\bigcup_{m\geq 0} Z_m$ is dense in Z. Hence for $s \in V$ and $\varepsilon > 0$ given there is a number $m \in \mathbb{N}$ and an element $\bar{s}_m \in Z_m$ such that

$$\|s - \bar{s}_m\|_Z < \varepsilon/(2+T).$$

Consequently,

$$s_m(t) = \bar{s}_m(t) + (s(0) - \bar{s}_m(0)) + (\dot{s}(0) - \dot{\bar{s}}_m(0))t, \quad t \in [0,T],$$

is in V and $\|s - s_m\|_Z < \varepsilon$ holds true. This proves that $\bigcup_{m \geq 0} (Z_m \cap V)$ is dense in V. So if we can show that $A^{(2)}$ has a nonempty interior $\mathring{A}^{(2)}$ relative to V, we can apply Lemma 2.1, and everything is proved then. For that we shall demonstrate that $s_0(t) = b + dt$ is element of $\mathring{A}^{(2)}$.

Let K = b if b > 0 and K = d if b = 0. Further, let $\varepsilon > 0$ be given such that

$$\varepsilon \leq \min\{K, C - (b + dT), (C - dT)/T\}.$$

Then for every $z \in V$ with $\|s_0 - z\|_Z \leq \varepsilon$ we have in case b > 0

$$C \geq b + dT + \varepsilon \geq s_0(t) + \varepsilon \geq z(t) \geq s_0(t) - \varepsilon \geq b - \varepsilon \geq 0$$

and in case b = 0

$$d + \varepsilon = \dot{s}_0(t) + \varepsilon \geq \dot{z}(t) \geq \dot{s}_0(t) - \varepsilon = d - \varepsilon \geq 0$$

which because of $s_0(0) = z(0) = 0$ implies

$$C \geq (d + \varepsilon)T \geq z(t) \geq (d - \varepsilon)t \geq 0$$

for all $t \in [0,T]$. Thus in any case z is in $A^{(2)}$. □

Let now $B \subset \mathbb{R}^2$ be the fixed part of the boundary of $\overline{D_T(\hat{s})}$ abbreviated by

$$B = \{t \in \mathbb{R} \mid 0 \leq t \leq T\} \cup \{x \in \mathbb{R} \mid 0 \leq x \leq b\}$$

and let Y be the product space

$$Y = C[0,T] \times C[0,b] \times C[0,T] \times C[0,T]$$

which is equipped with the norm

$$|||g|||_B = \max\{\|g_1\|_T, \|g_2\|_b, \|g_3\|_T, \|g_4\|_T\}$$

for $g = (g_1, g_2, g_3, g_4) \in Y$. Then we define an operator $T : (\bigcup_{n\geq 0} X_n(\mathbb{R}^2)) \times Z \to Y$ by

$$T(u,s) = (T_1(u) = u_x(0,\cdot),\ \ T_2(u) = u(\cdot,0),\ \ T_3(u,s) = \frac{d}{dt}u(s(\cdot),\cdot),$$
$$T_4(u,s) = u_x(s(\cdot),\cdot) + \dot{s}(\cdot)) \tag{12.14}$$

where "$\cdot$" stands for the independent variable t or x. (See Remark 12.2 (1) with regard to the definition of T_3. Further, note that in the following $X_n(\mathbb{R}^2)$ is not a normed space). If moreover

$$r = (r_1 = c,\ \ r_2 = f,\ \ r_3 = 0,\ \ r_4 = 0) \in Y,$$

for $n, m \in \mathbb{N}$ fixed we can state the nonlinear Chebyshev type approximation problem

$$(P_{n,m})\quad \text{Minimize } |||r - T(u,s)|||_B \text{ on } (X_n(\mathbb{R}^2) \cap A^{(1)}(\mathbb{R}^2)) \times (Z_m \cap A^{(2)}),$$

which has a minimal value $\rho_{n,m}$.

Let, furthermore, $\{B_k\}_{k\in\mathbb{N}}$ be a sequence of subsets of B which fulfills Assumption 8.1 and (8.15) and let

$$A_k^{(2)} = \{s \in V|\ \ 0 \le s(t) \le C \ \text{ for all } t \in B_k\} \tag{12.15}$$

with V (12.11). Then for every pair $n, m \in \mathbb{N}$ we can define the following 'discretized' version of $(P_{n,m})$ where the definition of $|||\cdot|||_{B_k}$ is clear from the context:

$$(P_{n,m}^k)\quad \text{Minimize } |||r-T(u,s)|||_{B_k} \text{ on } (X_n(\mathbb{R}^2) \cap A^{(1)}(\mathbb{R}^2)) \times (Z_m \cap A_k^{(2)}).$$

Let $\rho_{n,m}^k$ be the minimal value of $(P_{n,m}^k)$.

Before we are going to present the main theorem of this section, we provide the following lemma concerning Assumption 8.2.

<u>Lemma 12.2.</u> Let $m \in \mathbb{N}$. Then $\{A_k^{(2)}\}_{k\in\mathbb{N}}$ fulfills Assumptions 8.2 (i) and (ii) (with X_n replaced by Z_m) where $A^{(2)}$ and $A_k^{(2)}$ are defined by (12.12) and (12.15) and B_k, $k\in\mathbb{N}$, is assumed to include at least $m+1$ points of $[0,T]$.

Proof. We can proceed here as in the proof of Lemma 11.4 if we define

$$M_k = \{s \in (Z_m \cap V) \mid -\mu_k \le s(t) \le C + \mu_k \quad \text{for all } t \in [0,T]\}$$

with V (12.11) and if we replace y_0 there by $s_0(t) = b + dt$ here. We observe that for $m \ge 1$, s_0 is interior point of $Z_m \cap A^{(2)}$ relative to $Z_m \cap V$ (see the proof of Lemma 12.1). So it is easy to show, similarly as in the proof of Lemma 11.4, that there exists a number $\lambda_k \in (0,1]$ such that $s_0 + \lambda_k(s - s_0)$ is in $Z_m \cap A^{(2)}$ for all $s \in M_k$ with $k \in \mathbb{N}$ fixed.

In view of the computation of λ_k in case b = 0, we remark that by Lemma 11.3 there is a constant $\tilde{C}$ such that

$$\|s\|_Z \le \tilde{C} \quad \text{for all } s \in M_k \text{ and all } k \in \mathbb{N}.$$

Hence, in this case we can guarantee

$$d - \lambda_k(\tilde{C} + d) \le \dot{s}_0 + \lambda_k(\dot{s} - \dot{s}_0) \le d + \lambda_k(\tilde{C} - d)$$

for all $s \in M_k$ and $k \in \mathbb{N}$.

Now the remainder of the proof is straightforward. □

Theorem 12.1. Let $\bigcup_{n\ge 0} X_n(\overline{D_T(\hat{s})})$ be dense in X and let Assumption 12.1 be fulfilled. Further, define $\hat{u}(x,t) = 0$ for $x > \hat{s}(t)$ and $0 \le t \le T$. Then we have:

(1) If B_1 contains at least $n+1$ points of $[0,b]$ and $nm+1$ points of $[0,T]$, for each pair $n, m \in \mathbb{N}$ $(P_{n,m})$ and $(P^k_{n,m})$, $k \in \mathbb{N}$, possess solutions $(\hat{u}_n, \hat{s}_m)$ and $(\hat{u}^k_n, \hat{s}^k_m)$, respectively.

(2) $\lim_{n,m\to\infty} \rho_{n,m} = 0.$

(3) For n,m fixed, statements (1) - (3) of Theorem 8.1 (transferred to $(P_{n,m})$ and $(P^k_{n,m})$) are valid. In particular, $\lim_{k\to\infty} \rho^k_{n,m} = \rho_{n,m}$.

(4) For each couple $(u,s) \in (X_n(\mathbb{R}^2) \cap A^{(1)}(\mathbb{R}^2)) \times (Z_m \cap A^{(2)})$ with $n, m \in \mathbb{N}$, the following error bounds hold true, where H is given by (12.9):

(i) $\|\hat{s} - s\|_t \le (b + 2t + \max\{b + H(t)t,\ \|s\|_t\})\, |||r - T(u,s)|||_B$.

(ii) $|(\hat{u} - u)(x,t)| \le H(t)\|\hat{s} - s\|_t$

$+ (\max\{1,t\} + \|\hat{s} - s\|_t + \|s\|_t - x)\, |||r - T(u,s)|||_B$

for all $(x,t) \in \overline{D_T(s)}$.

(5) (i) $\lim_{n,m\to\infty} \|\hat{s} - \hat{s}_m\|_T = 0$ (where $\hat{s}_m$ depends on n),

(ii) $\lim_{n,m\to\infty} \|\hat{u} - \hat{u}_n\|_{\overline{D_T(\hat{s}_m)}} = 0.$

Proof. (1) and (3). Let n and m be fixed. We first observe that we have $|s(t)| \le C$ on B_k for all $s \in (Z_m \cap A_k^{(2)})$. Thus, by Lemma 11.3 there is a constant $K \ge C$ (depending on m) so that

$$\max\{\|s\|_T,\ \|\dot{s}\|_T,\ \|\ddot{s}\|_T\} \le K \text{ for all } s \in (Z_m \cap A_k^{(2)}) \text{ and all } k \in \mathbb{N}. \quad (12.16)$$

(12.16) implies in particular that all points $(s(t),t)$, $t \in [0,T]$, with $s \in (Z_m \cap A_k^{(2)})$, $k \in \mathbb{N}$, lie in the rectangle

$$E = \{(x,t) \in \mathbb{R}^2 \mid -K \le x \le K,\ \ 0 \le t \le T\}. \quad (12.17)$$

Further, we have $(s(t),t) \in E$ for each $s \in (Z_m \cap A^{(2)})$ and $t \in [0,T]$. Therefore, recalling the inclusion property of $\{A_k\}_{k\in\mathbb{N}}$ (cf. Lemma 12.2), for n,m fixed we could likewise define T as a mapping from $X_n(E) \times (Z_m \cap A_1^{(2)})$ into Y (given by (12.14)). This means that we could replace $X_n(\mathbb{R}^2)$ and $A^{(1)}(\mathbb{R}^2)$ in $(P_{n,m})$ and $(P^k_{n,m})$ by $X_n := X_n(E)$ and $A^{(1)} := A^{(1)}(E)$, respectively. For technical reasons we perform this here and provide X_n with the norm

$$\|u\|_{X_n} = \max\{\|u\|_E,\ \|u_x\|_E,\ \|u_t\|_E\}.$$

Our objective is now to prove the boundedness of the level sets

$$C_\alpha^k((X_n \cap A^{(1)}) \times (Z_m \cap A_k^{(2)}))$$
$$= \{(u,s) \in (X_n \cap A^{(1)}) \times (Z_m \cap A_k^{(2)}) \mid\ |||T(u,s)|||_{B_k} \le \alpha\} \quad (12.18)$$

in $X_n \times Z$ with respect to the product norm $\max\{\|u\|_{X_n}, \|s\|_Z\}$. For that let $k \in \mathbb{N}$ and $\alpha > 0$ be fixed.

For $u \in X_n$ there are reals $a_0, a_1, \ldots, a_n$ so that

$$u(x,t) = \sum_{i=0}^{n} a_i \, v_i(x,t). \tag{12.19}$$

Let us first consider the case $b > 0$. Then remembering (12.13), we obtain for each element (u,s) of (12.18)

$$\max_{x \in B_k} |u(x,0)| = \max_{x \in B_k} \left| \sum_{i=0}^{n} a_i x^i \right| \le \alpha$$

which by a standard argument (see e.g. the proof of Lemma 11.3) implies the uniform boundedness of all such u in X_n. Hence, recollecting (12.16), we have proved the boundedness of (12.18) for $b > 0$.

So we set $b = 0$. Then we have $d > 0$ such that $s \in (Z_m \cap A_k^{(2)})$ is a polynomial of degree p with $1 \le p \le m$. If now $q \in \{1,\ldots,n\}$ is the largest index such that $a_q \ne 0$, then the polynomial

$$\sum_{i=0}^{n} a_i \, v_i(s(t),t) = a_0 + a_1 \, s(t) + a_2(s^2(t) + 2t) + \ldots + a_q(s^q(t) + \ldots)$$

has the degree pq, $1 \le pq \le mn$, and hence cannot vanish on all of B_k by virtue of our assumptions on B_k. Consequently, for each $s \in (Z_m \cap A_k^{(2)})$ the functions $v_0(s(\cdot),\cdot), \ldots, v_n(s(\cdot),\cdot)$ are linearly independent on B_k. We shall make use of this fact in the proof of the boundedness of the set

$$Q_\alpha^k = \{(u,s) \in (X_n \cap A^{(1)}) \times (Z_m \cap A_k^{(2)}) \mid \max_{t \in B_k} |u_x(s(t),t) + \dot{s}(t)| \le \alpha\}$$

in $X_n \times Z$, which is our next aim. Obviously Q_α^k contains the set (12.18).

If we let $a^0 = (0, a_1, \ldots, a_n)$, $a^0 \ne 0$, and use $v_{i x} = i v_{i-1}$ for all $i \in \mathbb{N}$, we can conclude from (12.16) and (12.19) that

$$\max_{t \in B_k} |u_x(s(t),t)| = \|a^0\|_1 \max_{t \in B_k} \left| \sum_{i=1}^{n} \frac{a_i}{\|a^0\|_1} i v_{i-1}(s(t),t) \right| \le \alpha + K \tag{12.20}$$

for all $(u,s) \in Q_\alpha^k$. Further, we notice that the mapping

$$s \to \min_{\|a^0\|_1=1} \max_{t\in B_k} |\sum_{i=1}^{n} a_i\, i\, v_{i-1}(s(t),t)|$$

is continuous on $C^1[0,T]$. (To verify this, one can employ formula (2.14), p. 267, of DEM'YANOV/MALOZEMOV [74]). Since eventually $Z_m \cap A_k^{(2)}$ is a closed and by (12.16) a compact set in Z,

$$\mu = \inf\{ \min_{\|a^0\|_1=1} \max_{t\in B_k} |\sum_{i=1}^{n} a_i\, i\, v_{i-1}(s(t),t)| \,|\, s \in (Z_m \cap A_k^{(2)})\}$$

is achieved for a $s \in (Z_m \cap A_k^{(2)})$.

Due to the linear independence of $v_0(s(\cdot),\cdot),\ldots,v_n(s(\cdot),\cdot)$ on $Z_m \cap A_k^{(2)}$), μ is a positive number and hence (12.20) yields $\|a^0\|_1 \le (\alpha + K)/\mu$. This implies further the uniform boundedness of $\|a\|_1$, where $a = (a_0, a_1,\ldots,a_n)$, since a_0 is determined by $a_1,\ldots,a_n$ for each $u \in (X_n \cap A^{(1)})$. Consequently, by (12.16) Q_α^k and (12.18) are bounded sets in $X_n \times Z$. Moreover, T is continuous on $X_n \times (Z_m \cap A_1^{(2)})$. So if we transfer Lemma 8.2 to the present situation (see Remark 8.3 and note that the definition of $C_{\alpha_0}((X_n \cap A^{(1)}) \times (Z_m \cap A^{(2)}))$ is evident by (12.18)), we can arrive at statement (1).

Hence for each $k \in \mathbb{N}$ $(P_{n,m}^k)$ possesses a solution $(\hat{u}_n^k, \hat{s}_m^k) \in (X_n(E) \cap A^{(1)}(E)) \times (Z_m \cap A_k^{(2)})$. (Note that $\hat{u}_n^k$ is defined on all of $\mathbb{R}^2$). Further, we have just shown that after some modifications Lemma 8.2 can be applied here. Thus, recalling Lemma 12.2 and Remark 8.3, we still have to verify the equicontinuity of $\{T_i(\hat{u}_n^k)\}_{k\in\mathbb{N}}$ for i = 1,2 and of $\{T_i(\hat{u}_n^k, \hat{s}_m^k)\}_{k\in\mathbb{N}}$ for i = 3,4 on $[0,T]$ and $[0,b]$, respectively, in order to be able to employ Theorem 8.1 here. We shall perform this now for the case i = 3. The proofs for the cases i = 1,2,4 are similar.

By Lemma 8.2 (3), modified for the present situation, there exist constants γ_1 and γ_2 such that for all $k \in \mathbb{N}$ $\|\hat{s}_m^k\|_Z \le \gamma_1$ and $\|\hat{u}_n^k\|_{X_n} \le \gamma_2$ hold true. Using arguments as for Lemma 11.3 (see also (12.16)), we can conclude that there are constants K and L so that

$$\max\{\|\hat{s}_m^k\|_T, \|\dot{\hat{s}}_m^k\|_T, \|\ddot{\hat{s}}_m^k\|_T\} \le K \quad \text{for all } k \in \mathbb{N} \tag{12.21}$$

and

$$\max_{\substack{0\le i+j\le 2\\ i,j\in\{0,1,2\}}} \max_{(x,t)\in E} \left|\frac{\partial^{i+j}}{\partial x^i\,\partial t^j}\hat{u}_n^k(x,t)\right| \le L \quad \text{for all } k\in\mathbb{N}. \tag{12.22}$$

Let now $t,\ \tau\in[0,T]$. Then applying Taylor's theorem and using (12.21) and (12.22), we obtain

$$\begin{aligned}
&|[T_3(\hat{u}_n^k,\hat{s}_m^k)](t)-[T_3(\hat{u}_n^k,\hat{s}_m^k)](\tau)|\\
&= |\hat{u}^k_{n_x}(\hat{s}_m^k(t),t)\dot{\hat{s}}_m^k(t)+\hat{u}^k_{n_t}(\hat{s}_m^k(t),t)-\hat{u}^k_{n_x}(\hat{s}_m^k(\tau),\tau)\dot{\hat{s}}_m^k(\tau)-\hat{u}^k_{n_t}(\hat{s}_m^k(\tau),\tau)|\\
&\le |\hat{u}^k_{n_x}(\hat{s}_m^k(t),t)|\ |\dot{\hat{s}}_m^k(t)-\dot{\hat{s}}_m^k(\tau)|+|\hat{u}^k_{n_x}(\hat{s}_m^k(t),t)-\hat{u}^k_{n_x}(\hat{s}_m^k(\tau),\tau)|\ |\dot{\hat{s}}_m^k(\tau)|\\
&\qquad +|\hat{u}^k_{n_t}(\hat{s}_m^k(t),t)-\hat{u}^k_{n_t}(\hat{s}_m^k(\tau),\tau)|\\
&\le KL|t-\tau|+KL|\hat{s}_m^k(t)-\hat{s}_m^k(\tau)|+KL|t-\tau|\\
&\qquad +L|\hat{s}_m^k(t)-\hat{s}_m^k(\tau)|+L|t-\tau|\\
&\le L(3K+K^2+1)|t-\tau|.
\end{aligned}$$

(2). Since $K\ge C$, $(s(t),t)$ is in E (12.17) for all $s\in(Z_m\cap A^{(2)})$, $m\in\mathbb{N}$, and $t\in[0,T]$. Therefore, in order to consider $(P_{n,m})$ for $n,m\to\infty$, we can again redefine the domain of T for technical reasons without causing damage. So we let T be the operator from $(\bigcup_{n\ge0}(X_n(E)\cap A^{(1)}(E))\times(\bigcup_{m\ge0}(Z_m\cap A^{(2)}))$ into Y, which is determined by (12.14), and replace $X_n(\mathbb{R}^2)$ and $A^{(1)}(\mathbb{R}^2)$ in $(P_{n,m})$ by $X_n(E)$ and $A^{(1)}(E)$, respectively.

Now we shall first prove that for $\varepsilon>0$ given there are numbers n_0, $m_0\in\mathbb{N}$ and a couple $(u^*,s^*)\in(X_{n_0}(E)\cap A^{(1)}(E))\times(Z_{m_0}\cap A^{(2)})$ such that

$$|||r-T(u^*,s^*)|||_B<\varepsilon. \tag{12.23}$$

For that we choose $\varepsilon>0$ and fix $\theta>0$ so that

$$\max(3\theta,3\theta\|\hat{s}\|_Z+2\theta+2\theta^2)<\varepsilon.$$

Then, since $\bigcup_{n\geq 0} (X_n(\overline{D_T(\hat{s})}) \cap A^{(1)}(\overline{D_T(\hat{s})})$ is dense in $X \cap A^{(1)}(\overline{D_T(\hat{s})})$, we can find a number $n_0 \in \mathbb{N}$ and an element $u^* \in (X_{n_0}(\overline{D_T(\hat{s})}) \cap A^{(1)}(\overline{D_T(\hat{s})})$ such that

$$\|\hat{u} - u^*\|_X < \theta. \tag{12.24}$$

(12.24) immediately implies

$$\max\{\|r_1 - T_1(u^*)\|_T, \ \|r_2 - T_2(u^*)\|_b\} < \varepsilon. \tag{12.25}$$

u^* is a polynomial and hence defined on E. Let $\omega(u_x^*,\delta)$ and $\omega(u_t^*,\delta)$ be the moduli of continuity of u_x^* and u_t^* on E (see (8.7)). Then we select $\delta < \theta$ sufficiently small such that

$$\max\{\omega(u_x^*,\delta), \ \omega(u_t^*,\delta)\} < \theta. \tag{12.26}$$

Moreover, by Lemma 12.1 there is a number $m_0 \in \mathbb{N}$ and an element $s^* \in (Z_{m_0} \cap A^{(2)})$ with

$$\|\hat{s} - s^*\|_Z < \delta. \tag{12.27}$$

Hence, from (12.24), (12.26), and (12.27) we obtain

$$\begin{aligned}\|r_4 - T_4(u^*,s^*)\|_T &= \|u_x^*(s^*(\cdot),\cdot) + \dot{s}^* - \hat{u}_x(\hat{s}(\cdot),\cdot) - \dot{\hat{s}}\|_T \\ &\leq \|u_x^*(s^*(\cdot),\cdot) - u_x^*(\hat{s}(\cdot),\cdot)\|_T + \|u_x^*(\hat{s}(\cdot),\cdot) - \hat{u}_x(\hat{s}(\cdot),\cdot)\|_T + \|s^* - \hat{s}\|_Z \\ &< \omega(u_x^*,\delta) + \theta + \delta \leq 3\theta < \varepsilon.\end{aligned} \tag{12.28}$$

Similarly we can derive

$$\begin{aligned}\|r_3 - T_3(u^*,s^*)\|_T &= \|u_x^*(s^*(\cdot),\cdot)\dot{s}^* + u_t^*(s^*(\cdot),\cdot) - \hat{u}_x(\hat{s}(\cdot),\cdot)\dot{\hat{s}} - \hat{u}_t(\hat{s}(\cdot),\cdot)\|_T \\ &\leq \|\hat{u}_x(\hat{s}(\cdot),\cdot)\|_T \ \|\dot{s}^* - \dot{\hat{s}}\|_T + \|u_x^*(s^*(\cdot),\cdot) - u_x(\hat{s}(\cdot),\cdot)\|_T \ \|\dot{s}^*\|_T \\ &\quad + \|u_t^*(s^*(\cdot),\cdot) - \hat{u}_t(\hat{s}(\cdot),\cdot)\|_T \\ &\leq \|\dot{\hat{s}}\|_T\delta + (\omega(u_x^*,\delta) + \theta) \ \|\dot{s}^*\|_T + \omega(u_t^*,\delta) + \theta\end{aligned}$$

$$\leq \|\hat{s}\|_Z \delta + 2\theta(\|s^* - \hat{s}\|_Z + \|\hat{s}\|_Z) + 2\theta$$

$$\leq \|\hat{s}\|_Z(\delta + 2\theta) + 2\delta\theta + 2\theta) < \varepsilon. \qquad (12.29)$$

Combination of (12.25), (12.28), and (12.29) yields (12.23).

Further, if n_1, n_2, m_1 and m_2 are natural numbers with $n_2 \geq n_1$ and $m_2 \geq m_1$, we have $0 \leq \rho_{n_2,m_2} \leq \rho_{n_1,m_1}$. Thus for any choice of numbers n, m with $n \to \infty$ and $m \to \infty$ the sequence $\{\rho_{n,m}\}_{n,m \in \mathbb{N}}$ possesses a limit ρ^*. Since, moreover, we can conclude from (12.23) that for $n \geq n_0$ and $m \geq m_0$

$$0 \leq \rho_{n,m} \leq \rho_{n_0,m_0} \leq |||r - T(u^*,s^*)|||_B < \varepsilon$$

holds true, we can finally infer that ρ^* is identical zero.

(4). The inequality (i) follows readily from Theorem 3.1 of KNABNER [83].

In view of the proof of (ii), we notice first that $(\bar{u},\bar{s}) \in (X_n(\mathbb{R}^2) \cap A^{(1)}(\mathbb{R}^2)) \times (Z_m \cap A^{(2)})$ satisfies the equations (14.7-12) if $\beta_1 = 0$ and $\beta_2 = 1$ and

$$\rho_1 = T_1(\bar{u}) - r_1, \quad \rho_2 = T_2(\bar{u}) - r_2,$$

$$\dot{\rho}_3 = T_3(\bar{u},\bar{s}) - r_3, \quad \rho_4 = T_4(\bar{u},\bar{s}) - r_4.$$

Next we observe that for $\bar{u} \in (X_n(\mathbb{R}^2) \cap A^{(1)}(\mathbb{R}^2))$ we have $\rho_3(0) = \bar{u}(b,0) = 0$ and hence

$$\|\rho_3\|_t \leq \|\dot{\rho}_3\|_t t.$$

Thus we can deduce (ii) from Theorem 14.1 where we note that assumption (14.19) is not needed for its proof.

(5). Due to (1), for $n, m \in \mathbb{N}$ $(P_{n,m})$ possesses a solution $(\hat{u}_n,\hat{s}_m) \in (X_n(\mathbb{R}^2) \cap A^{(1)}(\mathbb{R}^2)) \times (Z_m \cap A^{(2)})$. Since $\hat{s}_m$, $m \in \mathbb{N}$, is element of $A^{(2)}$, we have $\|\hat{s}_m\|_T \leq C$ for all $m \in \mathbb{N}$. Thus (i) is an implication of (2) and (4) (i).

Finally, from (4) we conclude for $(\hat{u}_n, \hat{s}_m)$ that

$$|(\hat{u}-\hat{u}_n)(x,t)| \le [H(T)+\rho_{n,m}](b+2T+C)\rho_{n,m}+[\max(1,T)+C]\rho_{n,m} \tag{12.30}$$

holds true in $\overline{D_T(\hat{s}_m)}$, where we used (12.10). Thus by (2) we can force the right-hand side of (12.30) to become smaller than any prescribed $\varepsilon > 0$ if we select n and m sufficiently large. Hence, the proof of the theorem is complete. □

Remarks 12.2. (1) With minor modifications a theorem similar to Theorem 12.1 can be proved if $T_3(u,s)$ here is replaced by $T_3(u,s) = u(s(\cdot),\cdot)$. In this case one has to employ the bound on $\|\hat{s}-s\|_t$ from Theorem 14.2. However, we note that the bound derived by KNABNER [83] makes our method particularly attractive.

(2) The approach presented here can be easily extended to more general Stefan problems as long as that problem is well-posed. In this connection we refer again to the quite general stability theorem by KNABNER [83] (see also FASANO/PRIMICERIO [77a,b,c]).

(3) Numerical examples for the method under consideration have been given by REEMTSEN and LOZANO [81] and REEMTSEN [82a]. Furthermore, the method has been successfully applied to the numerical solution of partial problems in REEMTSEN and KIRSCH [84].

(4) A variety of other methods for the numerical solution of one-dimensional Stefan problems has been developed in the past. A comparative study and a list of references can be found in FURZELAND [80]. In addition to the methods discussed by FURZELAND, we would like to mention the one which is suggested by BAUMEISTER, HOFFMANN, and JOCHUM [80] (in this connection see also KRUEGER [82]).

13. AN ILL-POSED PROBLEM FOR THE HEAT EQUATION: THE INVERSE STEFAN PROBLEM

In this section we want to apply our method to the so-called 'inverse Stefan problem' and thereby show that it is very well suited for the 'solution' of ill-posed problems.

We begin with the formulation of the problem. For that let generally $x = (x_1,\ldots,x_r)$ denote a point in Euclidean r space $\mathbb{R}^r$. Although we are primarily interested in the case of one or two space dimensions in view of the numerical realization of the method, little extra effort is involved to present our results for the general case of r, $r \geq 1$, space dimensions and hence we shall do so.

For $0 < t \leq T < \infty$ let $\Omega(t)$ be a bounded connected domain in $\mathbb{R}^r$ with boundary $\partial\Omega(t) = \Gamma(t) \cup \Sigma(t)$ and assume $\Omega = \bigcup_{0<t\leq T} \{(x,t) \in \mathbb{R}^{r+1} \mid x \in \Omega(t)\}$ is a connected region in $\mathbb{R}^{r+1}$. Then the boundary $\partial\Omega$ of Ω consists of the 'bottom' $\overline{\Omega(0)}$, the 'top' $\overline{\Omega(T)}$, and the lateral surface $\bar{\Gamma} \cup \bar{\Sigma}$ where the 'free' boundary is $\Sigma = \bigcup_{0<t<T} \Sigma(t)$ and the 'fixed' boundary is $\Gamma = \bigcup_{0<t<T} \Gamma(t)$. Γ is simply connected whereas Σ may be multiply connected. We further assume that $\bar{\Sigma}$ is nowhere characteristic, i.e. that the spatial components of the normal to $\bar{\Sigma}$ never vanish simultaneously at any point of $\bar{\Sigma}$.

Moreover, we require roughly speaking that the geodetic and the Euclidean distance on (the connected region) $\bar{\Gamma} \cup \overline{\Omega(0)} \cup \bar{\Sigma}$ are equivalent, i.e. that there exists a constant $\gamma > 0$ such that for the length $d_g[(x,t), (\xi,\tau)]$ of any geodetic curve on $\bar{\Gamma} \cup \overline{\Omega(0)} \cup \bar{\Sigma}$ connecting two points (x,t) and (ξ,τ)

$$d_g[(x,t), (\xi,\tau)] \leq \gamma \|(x,t)-(\xi,\tau)\|_2 \quad \text{for all } (x,t), (\xi,\tau) \in \bar{\Gamma} \cup \overline{\Omega(0)} \cup \bar{\Sigma} \tag{13.1}$$

holds true where $\|\cdot\|_2$ is the Euclidean norm in $\mathbb{R}^{r+1}$. (The reversed inequality is always valid). Obviously, (13.1) is true for any surface $\bar{\Gamma} \cup \overline{\Omega(0)} \cup \bar{\Sigma}$ that is not pathological. Note that from (13.1) and the boundedness of Ω we get in particular the existence of a constant L_0 such that

$$d_g[(x,t), (\xi,\tau)] \leq L_0 \quad \text{for all } (x,t), (\xi,\tau) \in \bar{\Gamma}. \tag{13.2}$$

Besides we shall assume that $\partial\Omega$ is sufficiently smooth (cf. Assumption 13.4 below). Finally, let us say that by $C^{p,q}$ we denote again the space of functions which are p times continuously differentiable with respect to the space variables and q times continuously differentiable with respect to the time variable.

<u>Assumption 13.1.</u> Let $f \in C^1(\overline{\Omega(0)})$, $g \in C^1(\bar{\Sigma})$, and $h \in C(\bar{\Sigma})$ be given data which are compatible, i.e. for which in particular $f = g$ on $\overline{\Omega(0)} \cap \bar{\Sigma}$.

Then we consider here the following inverse Stefan problem. Given f, g, and h as in Assumption 13.1, find $u \in C^{2,1}(\Omega) \cap C^{1,0}(\bar{\Omega}) \cap C^{0,1}(\bar{\Gamma})$ (and thereby $c := u_{|\bar{\Gamma}}$) such that

$$\Delta_r u - u_t = 0 \quad \text{in } \Omega, \tag{13.3}$$

$$u = c \quad \text{on } \bar{\Gamma}, \tag{13.4}$$

$$u = f \quad \text{on } \overline{\Omega(0)}, \tag{13.5}$$

$$u = g \quad \text{on } \bar{\Sigma}, \tag{13.6}$$

$$\frac{\partial u}{\partial \nu} = h \quad \text{on } \bar{\Sigma}, \tag{13.7}$$

where ν is the normal with respect to the space variables that points into the region Ω. The initial condition (13.5) is omitted if $\overline{\Omega(0)}$ has dimension less than or equal to $r-1$.

It is well-known that the inverse Stefan problem has in general no solution even if Σ is analytic (see COLTON [74, 80]) and that in case it has a solution it does not depend continuously on the data (see e.g. CANNON/DOUGLAS [67a], HILL [67], PUCCI [59]). Hence one objective is to define what we mean by a 'solution' of (13.3-7) and to show that under suitable restrictions this 'solution' depends continuously on the given data. In order to do this, we shall write problem (13.3-7) in the fashion of our model problem (P), and we shall accomplish this in such a way that the problems (P_n) become linear approximation problems which are easily solvable.

We summarize and extend here the results of REEMTSEN and KIRSCH [84] and COLTON and REEMTSEN [84]. Let us note that for r = 1 JOCHUM [78, 80] and KNABNER [83a, 85] gave other formulations of a 'solution' of (13.3-7) and likewise suggested minimizing the defects in the corresponding operator equations. However, while for the solution of the one-dimensional inverse Stefan problem a variety of methods has been developed, by our knowledge COLTON and REEMTSEN [84] present the only acceptable numerical results for the case r = 2. (For more references on the inverse Stefan problem and its numerical 'solution', the reader is referred to JOCHUM [78], KNABNER [83a], REEMTSEN/KIRSCH [84], and COLTON/REEMTSEN [84]).

We start now with defining a normed space X by

$$X = \{u \in C^{2,1}(\Omega) \cap C^{1,0}(\bar{\Omega}) \cap C^{1,0}(\bar{\Gamma}) \mid \Delta_r u - u_t = 0 \text{ in } \Omega\}$$

and

$$\|u\|_X = \max_{1 \le i \le r} \{\|u\|_{\bar{\Omega}}, \|u_{x_i}\|_{\bar{\Omega}}, \|u_t\|_{\bar{\Gamma}}\}$$

where $\|\cdot\|_D$ denotes the supremum norm on $D \subseteq \mathbb{R}^{r+1}$. In order to incorporate constraints on $u_{|\bar{\Gamma}}$ which, for instance, may guarantee the unique solvability of the corresponding direct Stefan problem with data $u_{|\bar{\Gamma}}$, f, g, and h, let E be an appropriate subset of X. Motivated by the one-dimensional case (cf. Sect. 14.2), we confine ourselves here to the examples

$$E = X \quad \text{or} \quad E = \{u \in X \mid \ u \ge 0 \text{ on } \bar{\Gamma}\}. \tag{13.8}$$

Furthermore, we choose Y to be the product space

$$Y = C(\overline{\Omega(0)}) \times C(\bar{\Sigma}) \times C(\bar{\Sigma})$$

and supply Y with the norm

$$|||y|||_{\overline{\Omega(0)} \cup \bar{\Sigma}} = \max\{\|y_1\|_{\overline{\Omega(0)}}, \ \|y_2\|_{\bar{\Sigma}}, \ \|y_3\|_{\bar{\Sigma}}\}$$

for $y = (y_1, y_2, y_3) \in Y$. Then we can define an operator $T : X \to Y$ by

$$Tu = (T_1 u = u_{|\overline{\Omega(0)}}, \ T_2 u = u_{|\bar{\Sigma}}, \ T_3 u = \frac{\partial u}{\partial \nu}_{|\bar{\Sigma}}).$$

(The domains of definition of $T_i u$, $i = 1,2,3$, are given for the sake of comprehension). Obviously T is linear and continuous. So if Assumption 13.1 is fulfilled and

$$r = (r_1 = f, \ r_2 = g, \ r_3 = h) \in Y,$$

we can state the above inverse Stefan problem as follows:

(ISP) Find $u \in E$ such that $Tu = r$.

We note again that in case $\overline{\Omega(0)}$ has dimension less than or equal to $r - 1$ all terms related to $\overline{\Omega(0)}$ above have to be omitted.

In order to ensure convergence of our method in case (ISP) has a unique solution, we next formulate the following assumption.

Assumption 13.2. (ISP) possesses a unique solution $u^* \in E$ for which a constant M is known such that

$$\max_{1\le i\le r} \{\|u^*_{x_i}\|_{\bar{\Gamma}}, \ \|u^*_t\|_{\bar{\Gamma}}\} < M. \tag{13.9}$$

Let now E (13.8) and $M > 0$ be given. Motivated by (13.9), we then define A to be any subset of

$$\{u \in E \mid \max_{1\le i\le r} (\|u_{x_i}\|_{\bar{\Gamma}}, \ \|u_t\|_{\bar{\Gamma}}) \le M\}$$

with the following properties: First, A is a closed convex subset of a linear variety $V \subseteq X$ and has a nonempty interior $\mathring{A}$ relative to V in X; and secondly, u^* is in A in case Assumption 13.2 is satisfied. Thus, we can use A for storing further a priori information on the solution of (ISP) (if it exists). In particular,

$$A = \{u \in E \mid \max_{1\le i\le r} (\|u_{x_i}\|_{\bar{\Gamma}}, \ \|u_t\|_{\bar{\Gamma}}) \le M\} \tag{13.10}$$

(with V = X) is a possible choice for A.

We now replace (ISP) by the regularized problem

(P) Find $u \in A$ such that $Tu = r$

which has the form of our general problem in Sect. 1 and possesses the unique solution $u^* \in E$ if Assumption 13.2 is fulfilled. Hence, we can proceed as before and assume first the following.

Assumption 13.3. $\{v_n\}_{n\in\mathbb{N}}$ is a family of functions in X such that $\bigcup_{n\in\mathbb{N}} (X_n \cap V)$ is dense in V where $X_n = \langle v_1,\dots,v_n\rangle$ is an n-dimensional subspace of X and $v_1 = 1$. Moreover, v_i, $i \in \mathbb{N}$, has continuous partial derivatives of second order on $\bar{\Gamma} \cup \overline{\Omega(0)} \cup \bar{\Sigma}$.

Remark 13.1. If Ω is simply connected, for $r \in \mathbb{N}$ the heat polynomials or combinations of the heat polynomials form a family of solutions of the heat equation (13.3) which is complete in a certain sense (cf. Remark 12.1 and COLTON [80]). For doubly connected domains in Ω and $r = 2$, a family of solutions of (13.3) can be found in the paper of COLTON and REEMTSEN [84], who also describe how complete families of solutions can be constructed if Ω is multiply connected and $r \geq 2$. For all these families of functions, however, completeness in X has not been proved yet.

Concerning our general Assumption B, we can next state the following lemma which is evident by Lemma 2.1. (Note also that any positive constant is element of A (13.10)).

Lemma 13.1. If Assumption 13.3 is fulfilled, $\bigcup_{n \in \mathbb{N}} (X_n \cap A)$ is dense in A. Moreover, there exists a number $n_0 \in \mathbb{N}$ such that $X_n \cap A$ is nonempty for all $n \geq n_0$ where we have $n_0 = 1$ for A (13.10).

Hence, under Assumption 13.3 it is meaningful to consider the finite dimensional approximation problems

$$(P_n) \quad \text{Minimize } |||r - Tu|||_{\overline{\Omega(0)} \cup \bar{\Sigma}} \quad \text{on } X_n \cap A$$

for $n \geq n_0$. We denote the minimal value of (P_n) again by ρ_n.

In order to handle (P_n) numerically, we 'discretize' (P_n) for fixed n. For that let $B = \bar{\Gamma} \cup \overline{\Omega(0)} \cup \bar{\Sigma}$, and $\Gamma_k \subseteq \bar{\Gamma}$, $\Omega_k(0) \subseteq \overline{\Omega(0)}$, and $\Sigma_k \subseteq \bar{\Sigma}$ be compact sets such that $\{B_k\}_{k \in \mathbb{N}}$ with $B_k = \Gamma_k \cup \Omega_k(0) \cup \Sigma_k$ satisfies Assumption 8.1 and (8.15). Further, regarding (13.8) let

$$E_k = X \quad \text{or} \quad E_k = \{u \in X \mid \ u \geq 0 \ \text{ on } \Gamma_k\}, \tag{13.11}$$

respectively. Finally, we define $\{A_k\}_{k \in \mathbb{N}}$ to be a sequence of closed convex subsets of X for which Assumption 8.2 (i) and

$$A_k \subseteq \{u \in E_k \mid \max_{1 \leq i \leq r} (\|u_{x_i}\|_{\Gamma_k}, \|u_t\|_{\Gamma_k}) \leq M\}, \ k \in \mathbb{N},$$

hold true. So in particular for A (13.10), $\{A_k\}_{k \in \mathbb{N}}$ with

$$A_k = \{u \in E_k \mid \max_{1\le i\le r} (\|u_{x_i}\|_{\Gamma_k}, \|u_t\|_{\Gamma_k}) \le M\} \tag{13.12}$$

complies with the requirements by virtue of our assumptions on $\{B_k\}_{k\in\mathbb{N}}$.

We are now ready to give the following 'discretized' version of (P_n):

(P_n^k) Minimize $|||r - Tu|||_{\Omega_k(0)\cup\Sigma_k}$ on $X_n \cap A_k$

where (P_n^k) has a minimal value ρ_n^k. For the sequence $\{A_k\}_{k\in\mathbb{N}}$ we can now prove

<u>Lemma 13.2.</u> Let Assumption 13.3 be satisfied and let $n\in\mathbb{N}$ be fixed. Further, let $v_1,\dots,v_n$ be linearly independent on $\Sigma_{\bar{k}}$ for $\bar{k} = \bar{k}(n)\in\mathbb{N}$. Then (with regard to Remark 8.3) Assumptions 8.2 (i) and (ii)' are fulfilled for A (13.10) and A_k (13.12), where E and E_k are given by (13.8) and (13.11), respectively.

<u>Proof.</u> It remains to verify Assumption 8.2 (ii)'.

By Lemma 13.1, $X_n \cap A$ is nonempty for all $n\in\mathbb{N}$. So let u_0 be element of $X_n \cap A$ and

$$\alpha_0 = |||r|||_{\overline{\Omega(0)}\cup\bar{\Sigma}} + |||r - Tu_0|||_{\overline{\Omega(0)}\cup\bar{\Sigma}}.$$

Then we can define

$$C_{\alpha_0}(X_n \cap A) = \{u \in (X_n \cap A) \mid |||Tu|||_{\overline{\Omega(0)}\cup\bar{\Sigma}} \le \alpha_0\} \tag{13.13}$$

and

$$C_{\alpha_0}^k(X_n \cap A_k) = \{u \in (X_n \cap A_k) \mid |||Tu|||_{\Omega_k(0)\cup\Sigma_k} \le \alpha_0\}. \tag{13.14}$$

Since T is linear and continuous on X, (13.13) and (13.14) are convex and closed sets. Further, for $u \in C_{\alpha_0}^k(X_n \cap A_k)$ we have in particular

$$\|T_2 u\|_{\Sigma_k} = \|u\|_{\Sigma_k} \le \alpha_0.$$

Therefore, using arguments as in the proof of Lemma 11.3 and recalling (8.16) (which is also valid here), we can easily conclude that $C_{\alpha_0}(X_n \cap A)$ and $C^k_{\alpha_0}(X_n \cap A_k)$, $k \geq \bar{k}$, are bounded sets in X.

Moreover, we can obtain by an extension of Lemma 11.3 to functions on compact $B \subset \mathbb{R}^{r+1}$ that there is a constant K such that

$$\max_{\substack{0 \le i_i + \dots + i_r + j \le 2 \\ i_1,\dots,i_r,j \in \{0,1,2\}}} \left\| \frac{\partial^{i_1 + \dots + i_r + j}}{\partial x_1^{i_1} \dots \partial x_r^{i_r} \partial t^j} u(x,t) \right\|_{\bar{\Gamma} \cup \overline{\Omega(0)} \cup \bar{\Sigma}} \leq K \tag{13.15}$$

$$\text{for all } u \in C^k_{\alpha_0}(X_n \cap A_k) \text{ and all } k \geq \bar{k},$$

where we note that $u \in X_n$ possesses continuous partial derivatives of second order on $\bar{\Gamma} \cup \overline{\Omega(0)} \cup \bar{\Sigma}$ by virtue of Assumption 13.3.

If now C is any geodetic curve on $\bar{\Gamma}$ connecting two points $(x,t) \in \bar{\Gamma}$ and $(\xi,\tau) \in \bar{\Gamma}$, we can derive from (13.15) for $u \in C^k_{\alpha_0}(X_n \cap A_k)$, $k \geq \bar{k}$,

$$|u(x,t) - u(\xi,\tau)| = \left| \int_C \sum_{i=1}^{r} \frac{\partial}{\partial x_i} u(x,t) dx_i + \frac{\partial}{\partial t} u(x,t) dt \right|$$

$$\leq (r+1) K \gamma \, \|(x,t) - (\xi,\tau)\|_2$$

where we employed (13.1). We can similarly proceed for u_{x_i} and u_t on $\bar{\Gamma}$ and on (the connected region) $\overline{\Omega(0)} \cup \bar{\Sigma}$, respectively. Therefore, we can obtain in analogy to (11.18) in the proof of Lemma 11.4 that $C_{\alpha_0}(X_n \cap A) \subseteq C^k_{\alpha_0}(X_n \cap A_k) \subseteq N_k$ for all $k \geq \bar{k}$ and

$$N_k = \{u \in X_n | \quad u \geq -\mu_k \text{ on } \bar{\Gamma}, \quad \max_{1 \le i \le r} (\|u_{x_i}\|_{\bar{\Gamma}}, \|u_t\|_{\bar{\Gamma}}) \leq M + \mu_k,$$

$$|||Tu|||_{\overline{\Omega(0)} \cup \bar{\Sigma}} \leq \alpha_0 + \mu_k\} \tag{13.16}$$

holds true where $\mu_k \geq \mu_{k+1}$ and $\lim_{k\to\infty} \mu_k = 0$. The first restriction in (13.16) has to be omitted in case $E = E_k = X$.

Finally we observe that $u_0 = \delta$ with $\delta > 0$ is interior point of $X_n \cap A$ in X_n. (Note that $v_1 = 1$ by Assumption 13.3). Then the proof can be completed analogously to the proof of Lemma 11.4. □

Before we can state the main theorem of this section, we have to provide the following assumption.

Assumption 13.4. Let $\partial\Omega$ be sufficiently smooth and the data f, g, and h sufficiently regular such that for every $c \in C(\bar{\Gamma})$ satisfying

$$c = \begin{cases} f & \text{on } \bar{\Gamma} \cap \overline{\Omega(0)} \\ g & \text{on } \bar{\Gamma} \cap \bar{\Sigma} \end{cases}$$

the boundary value problems (13.3-6) and (13.3-5), (13.7) have unique solutions in $C(\bar{\Omega})$ which depend continuously on the data.

Remark 13.2. For r = 1 Assumption 13.4 can always be satisfied if the data are sufficiently smooth (see CANNON [84] and GEVREY [13] if $\dim \Omega(0) = 1$ and use STERNBERG [29] and a modification of Lemma 4 by SHERMAN [71] in case $\Omega(0)$ vanishes). In order to fulfill Assumption 13.4 for $r > 1$, one can appeal to Theorem 6.1 by LADYŽENSKAJA [67].

We are now in the position to give the following theorem.

Theorem 13.1. Let Assumptions 13.1 and 13.3 be satisfied and let $n \geq n_0$ with n_0 from Lemma 13.1. Moreover, let $v_1, \ldots, v_n$ be linearly independent on $\Sigma_{\bar{k}}$ for $\bar{k} = \bar{k}(n) \in \mathbb{N}$. Then the following statements are valid:

(1) (P_n) and (P_n^k), $k \geq \bar{k}$, possess solutions $\hat{u}_n \in (X_n \cap A)$ and $\hat{u}_n^k \in (X_n \cap A_k)$, respectively.

(2) If A (13.10) and A_k (13.12) are given, statements (1) - (3) of Theorem 8.1 hold here; in particular, we have $\lim_{k\to\infty} \rho_n^k = \rho_n$.

If in addition Assumptions 13.2 and 13.4 are fulfilled, then we also have

(3) $\lim_{n\to\infty} \rho_n = 0$.

(4) $\lim_{n\to\infty} \|u^* - \hat{u}_n\|_{\bar{\Omega}} = 0$.

Proof. At the beginning of the proof of Lemma 13.2 we have shown (without making use of the specifications of A and A_k in (13.10) and (13.12)) that $C_\alpha^k(X_n \cap A_k)$ is a bounded set in X for $k \geq \bar{k}$. Hence we can apply Lemma 8.2 in connection with Remark 8.3, and (1) is proved.

Statement (2) is a consequence of Theorem 8.1 in combination with Lemma 13.2, Theorem 8.2, Lemma 8.2, and Remark 8.3. Further, we can conclude (3) from Theorem 3.1 if we take Lemma 13.1 into consideration. Hence it remains to prove (4).

$X_n \cap A$ is nonempty for all $n \geq n_0$. So we can fix an element $u_0 \in (X_{n_0} \cap A)$ and obtain

$$|||r - T\hat{u}_n|||_{\overline{\Omega(0)} \cup \bar{\Sigma}} \leq |||r - Tu_0|||_{\overline{\Omega(0)} \cup \bar{\Sigma}} \quad \text{for all } n \geq n_0$$

where $\hat{u}_n$ is any solution of (P_n). Thus, using the definition of T, we can further conclude that there is a constant K such that

$$\|\hat{u}_n\|_{\overline{\Omega(0)} \cup \bar{\Sigma}} \leq K \quad \text{for all } n \geq n_0. \tag{13.17}$$

Next, let C be any geodetic curve on $\bar{\Gamma}$ which connects the points $(x,t) \in \bar{\Gamma}$ and $(\xi,\tau) \in \bar{\Gamma} \cap \overline{\Omega(0)}$. Then from (13.2), (13.10), and (13.17) we can derive that

$$\begin{aligned} |\hat{u}_n(x,t)| &\leq |\hat{u}_n(\xi,\tau)| + |\hat{u}_n(x,t) - \hat{u}_n(\xi,\tau)| \\ &= |\hat{u}_n(\xi,\tau)| + \left|\int_C \sum_{i=1}^r \frac{\partial}{\partial x_i} \hat{u}_n(x,t)dx_i + \frac{\partial}{\partial t}\hat{u}_n(x,t)dt\right| \\ &\leq K + (r+1)ML_0 \quad \text{for all } (x,t) \in \bar{\Gamma}, \end{aligned} \tag{13.18}$$

i.e. that all $c_n := \hat{u}_{n|\bar{\Gamma}}$, $n \geq n_0$, are uniformly bounded on $\bar{\Gamma}$. Similarly we can obtain from (13.1) that for all $(x,t) \in \bar{\Gamma}$, $(\xi,\tau) \in \bar{\Gamma}$, and for all $n \geq n_0$

$$|\hat{u}_n(x,t) - \hat{u}_n(\xi,\tau)| \leq (r+1)M_\gamma \|(x,t) - (\xi,\tau)\|_2$$

holds true. Thus the c_n are equicontinuous on $\bar{\Gamma}$, and we can conclude from the Arzela-Ascoli theorem that there exists a subsequence $\{c_{n(k)}\}_{k\in\mathbb{N}}$ of $\{c_n\}_{n\in\mathbb{N}}$ which converges uniformly to an element $\bar{c}$ of $C(\bar{\Gamma})$. Clearly, $\bar{c}$ is nonnegative on $\bar{\Gamma}$ if this is the case for all $c_{n(k)}$, $k \in \mathbb{N}$.

Now note that

$$\hat{u}_{n(k)} = \begin{cases} c_{n(k)} & \text{on } \bar{\Gamma}, \\ f + (\hat{u}_{n(k)} - f) & \text{on } \overline{\Omega(0)}, \\ g + (\hat{u}_{n(k)} - g) & \text{on } \bar{\Sigma}, \end{cases}$$

and, therefore,

$$c_{n(k)} = \begin{cases} f + (\hat{u}_{n(k)} - f) & \text{on } \bar{\Gamma} \cap \overline{\Omega(0)}, \\ g + (\hat{u}_{n(k)} - g) & \text{on } \bar{\Gamma} \cap \bar{\Sigma}. \end{cases}$$

So the convergence of $\{\rho_{n(k)}\}_{k\in\mathbb{N}}$ to zero (see (3)) and of $\{c_{n(k)}\}_{k\in\mathbb{N}}$ to $\bar{c}$ implies that $\bar{c}$ satisfies the compatibility condition of Assumption 13.4. Thus we know that the boundary value problems (13.3-6) and (13.3-5), (13.7) with data $\bar{c}$ on $\bar{\Gamma}$ have unique solutions $v \in C(\bar{\Omega})$ and $w \in C(\bar{\Omega})$, respectively.

Obviously $\hat{u}_{n(k)}$ satisfies the following equations:

$$\Delta_r \hat{u}_{n(k)} - \frac{\partial}{\partial t} \hat{u}_{n(k)} = 0 \quad \text{in } \Omega,$$

$$\hat{u}_{n(k)} = \bar{c} + (\hat{u}_{n(k)} - \bar{c}) \quad \text{on } \bar{\Gamma},$$

$$\hat{u}_{n(k)} = f + (\hat{u}_{n(k)} - f) \quad \text{on } \overline{\Omega(0)},$$

$$\hat{u}_{n(k)} = g + (\hat{u}_{n(k)} - g) \quad \text{on } \bar{\Sigma},$$

$$\frac{\partial}{\partial \nu} \hat{u}_{n(k)} = h + (\frac{\partial}{\partial \nu} \hat{u}_{n(k)} - h) \quad \text{on } \bar{\Sigma}.$$

Because of (3), the convergence of $\{c_{n(k)}\}_{k\in\mathbb{N}}$ to $\bar{c}$, and the continuous dependence of v and w on the data (see Assumption 13.4), we obtain $\hat{u}_{n(k)} \to v$ in $C(\bar{\Omega})$ and $\hat{u}_{n(k)} \to w$ in $C(\bar{\Omega})$ for $k \to \infty$. Thus we have $v = w$ and, moreover, $v = w = u^*$ and $\bar{c} = u^*_{|\bar{\Gamma}}$ by virtue of Assumption 13.2. Hence, every convergent subsequence of $\{c_n\}_{n\in\mathbb{N}}$ and so the sequence $\{c_n\}_{n\in\mathbb{N}}$ itself converges to $u^*_{|\bar{\Gamma}}$. Consequently, (4) is true, and the proof is complete. □

Remarks 13.3. (1) If we cannot guarantee that Assumption 13.2 is fulfilled, i.e. if we do not know whether or not a solution to the inverse Stefan problem exists, it follows from the proof of Theorem 13.1 (4) that there still exists a convergent subsequence $\{c_{n(k)}\}_{k\in\mathbb{N}}$ of $\{c_n\}_{n\in\mathbb{N}}$. The corresponding set $\{\hat{u}_{n(k)}\}_{k\in\mathbb{N}}$ defines a sequence of 'best approximations' in the set A in the sense that $\{\hat{u}_{n(k)}\}_{k\in\mathbb{N}}$ converges on $\bar{\Gamma}$ and optimally approximates the given data as k tends to infinity.

(2) In case $r = 1$, for every control $c_n := \hat{u}_{n|\bar{\Gamma}}$ there exists a classical solution $(\tilde{u}_n, \tilde{\Sigma}_n)$ to the corresponding 'direct' Stefan problem, and by using a stability result for the free boundaries it can be shown that the $\tilde{\Sigma}_n$ converge to Σ for $n \to \infty$ (see the following subsection). In the multidimensional case, however, a classical solution to the corresponding Stefan problem may not exist for large time intervals (for small time intervalls see MEIRMANOV [81]), and to our knowledge stability results for the free boundaries are unavailable.

(3) Numerical results of the method suggested here have been presented by REEMTSEN and KIRSCH [82, 84] for the case $r = 1$ and by COLTON and REEMTSEN [84] for the case $r = 2$.

13.1. THE CASE r = 1

We consider now the special situation where

$$r = 1,\ \bar{\Gamma} = \{(0,t) \in \mathbb{R}^2 \mid 0 \le t \le T\},\ \overline{\Omega(0)} = \{(x,0) \in \mathbb{R}^2 \mid 0 \le x \le b\} \text{ with}$$
$$b > 0, \text{ and } \bar{\Sigma} = \{(s(t),t) \in \mathbb{R}^2 \mid \ 0 \le t \le T\} \text{ where } s(0) = b. \qquad (13.19)$$

Then we specify here Assumption 13.1 as follows.

Assumption 13.5. In addition to (13.19) let $g \in C^1[0,T]$, $h \in C[0,T]$, $f \in C^2[0,b]$, and $s \in C^1[0,T]$ be given where f and s satisfy $f(x) \ge 0$ for all $x \in [0,b]$, $f(b) = g(0)$, and $s(t) > b$ for all $t \in [0,T]$.

Then under Assumption 13.5 our hypotheses on the region Ω and its boundary are obviously satisfied, and the equations (13.3-7) have here the following form:

$$Lu(x,t) := u_{xx}(x,t) - u_t(x,t) = 0 \quad \text{in } D_T(s) = \Omega, \tag{13.20}$$

$$u(0,t) = c(t), \qquad 0 \le t \le T, \tag{13.21}$$

$$u(x,0) = f(x), \qquad 0 \le x \le b = s(0), \tag{13.22}$$

$$u(s(t),t) = g(t), \qquad 0 \le t \le T, \tag{13.23}$$

$$u_x(s(t),t) = h(t), \qquad 0 \le t \le T, \tag{13.24}$$

where

$$D_T(s) := \Omega = \{(x,t) \in \mathbf{R}^2 \mid \ 0 < x < s(t), \ 0 < t \le T\}.$$

Our first aim now is to prove that under the assumptions of Theorem 13.1 (with Assumption 13.1 replaced by Assumption 13.5) the $c_n(\cdot) := \hat{u}_n(0,\cdot)$ generate unique solutions $(\tilde{u}_n, \tilde{s}_n)$ to the corresponding direct Stefan problems (13.20-24) with data c_n, f, g, and h, and that $\tilde{s}_n$ converges to s in $C[0,T]$ and $\tilde{u}_n$ to u^* in $C(\overline{D_T(s)})$. We shall accomplish this for the special case where the 'classical' Cauchy data

$$g(t) = 0 \quad \text{and} \quad h(t) = -\dot{s}(t) \quad \text{for } 0 \le t \le T \tag{13.25}$$

are given. However, the following theorem can be easily extended to more general situations as long as a stability result for the free boundary in the corresponding direct Stefan problem is available (for that see FASANO and PRIMICERIO [77a,b]).

We define the sets E and A here by

$$E = \{u \in X \mid \ u(0,t) \ge 0 \ \text{ for all } t \in [0,T]\} \tag{13.26}$$

and

$$A = \{u \in E \mid \ u(0,0) = f(0), \ \|u_t\|_{[0,T]} \le M\}. \tag{13.27}$$

Hence A is a closed convex subset of the linear variety

$$V = \{u \in X \mid \ u(0,0) = f(0)\} \tag{13.28}$$

of X and has a nonempty interior $\mathring{A}$ relative to V in X. (E.g. follow the last part of the proof of Lemma 12.1 in order to show that $f(0) + x^2 + Mt/2$ is element of $\mathring{A}$).

We further note that for the sequence $\{X_n\}_{n\in\mathbb{N}}$ of Assumption 13.3, $\bigcup_{n\in\mathbb{N}} (X_n \cap V)$ is dense in V (13.28) if and only if $\bigcup_{n\in\mathbb{N}} X_n$ is dense in X. Moreover, $X_n \cap A$ contains the constant f(0) for each $n \in \mathbb{N}$ and, therefore, is nonempty. With these definitions and observations we are now ready to prove the following theorem.

Theorem 13.2. Let Assumptions 13.5, 13.2, and 13.3 be satisfied where g, h, and E are given by (13.25) and (13.26), respectively. Then we have for $n \in \mathbb{N}$:

(1) (P_n) possesses a solution $\hat{u}_n \in (X_n \cap A)$ for A (13.27).

(2) The direct Stefan problem (13.20-24) with data $c_n(\cdot) := \hat{u}_n(0,\cdot)$, f, g, and h has a unique solution $(\tilde{u}_n, \tilde{s}_n) \in C^{2,1}(D_T(\tilde{s}_n)) \cap C^{0,0}(\overline{D_T(\tilde{s}_n)}) \times C^1[0,T]$.

(3) $\lim_{n\to\infty} \|s - \tilde{s}_n\|_{[0,T]} = 0$.

(4) $\lim_{n\to\infty} \|u^* - \tilde{u}_n\|_{\overline{D_T(s)}} = 0$.

Proof. We first observe that Assumption 13.5, which stands for Assumption 13.1 here, ensures that Assumption 13.4 is fulfilled (see e.g. CANNON [84] with respect to problem (13.20-23) and GEVREY [13] with respect to problem (13.20-22), (13.24) and note that by the results of GEVREY [13] in the latter case $f \in C^2[0,b]$ implies continuity of u_x and hence of u in the point (b,0)).

Next, we can conclude from the proof of Lemma 13.2 that $C_{\alpha_0}(X_n \cap A)$ is bounded and, therefore, statement (1) is a consequence of Theorem 5.2. Further, Assumption 14.3 of the Appendix is fulfilled here due to our assumptions on the data and the fact that $\hat{u}_n$ is in A (13.27). Thus, statement (2) has been verified (see Sect. 14.2.1).

With regard to statement (3) we notice that $(\tilde{u}_n, \tilde{s}_n) \in C^{2,1}(D_T(\tilde{s}_n)) \cap C^{0,0}(\overline{D_T(\tilde{s}_n)}) \times C^1[0,T]$ is a solution of

$$L\tilde{u}_n(x,t) = 0 \qquad \text{in } D_T(\tilde{s}_n),$$

$$\tilde{u}_n(0,t) = c_n(t), \qquad 0 \le t \le T,$$
$$\tilde{u}_n(x,0) = f(x), \qquad 0 \le x \le b = \tilde{s}_n(0),$$
$$\tilde{u}_n(\tilde{s}_n(t),t) = 0, \qquad 0 \le t \le T,$$
$$\tilde{u}_{n_x}(\tilde{s}_n(t),t) = -\dot{\tilde{s}}_n(t), \qquad 0 \le t \le T,$$

whereas $(\hat{u}_n, s) \in C^{2,1}(D_T(s)) \cap C^{0,0}(\overline{D_T(s)}) \times C^1[0,T]$ solves

$$L\,\hat{u}_n(x,t) = 0 \qquad \text{in } D_T(s),$$
$$\hat{u}_n(0,t) = c_n(t), \qquad 0 \le t \le T,$$
$$\hat{u}_n(x,0) = f(x) + [(T_1\hat{u}_n)(x) - f(x)], \qquad 0 \le x \le b = s(0),$$
$$\hat{u}_n(s(t),t) = (T_2\hat{u}_n)(t), \qquad 0 \le t \le T,$$
$$\hat{u}_{n_x}(s(t),t) = -\dot{s}(t) + [(T_3\hat{u}_n)(t) + \dot{s}(t)], \qquad 0 \le t \le T.$$

Obviously $(\tilde{u}_n, \tilde{s}_n)$ and $(\hat{u}_n, s)$ take the place of (u,s) and $(\bar{u},\bar{s})$ in Sect. 14.2.1. Thus, due to Theorem 13.1 (3), $(\hat{u}_n, s)$ satisfies Assumption 14.4 for all sufficiently large $n \in \mathbb{N}$. Hence we can conclude statement (3) from Theorem 14.4 if we take Theorem 13.1 (3) into account and bear in mind that $M(T)$ (14.28), depending on n here, is uniformly bounded for all $n \in \mathbb{N}$ (see (13.18)). Finally, employing Theorem 14.3, we arrive at

$$\lim_{n\to\infty} \|\tilde{u}_n - \hat{u}_n\|_{\overline{D_T(s)}} = 0,$$

which together with Theorem 13.1 (4) implies statement (4). □

At the end of this section we turn to a question which was raised by the numerical results of REEMTSEN and KIRSCH [82, 84] and COLTON and REEMTSEN [84]. The authors of these papers observed that, in case the data s, f (for $b > 0$), g, and h are analytic, the inverse Stefan problem possesses a solution, and $X_n = \langle v_0, v_1, \ldots, v_n \rangle$, where v_i is the heat polynomial (12.13) on $\overline{D_T(s)}$, $\hat{u}_n$ converges to u^* in $C(\bar{\Omega})$ even if no regularizing constraints are imposed on the problem, i.e even if $A = X_n$ in (P_n) (e.g. see Examples 1 in REEMTSEN/KIRSCH [84] and COLTON/REEMTSEN [84]). This observation is confusing since it is well-known that convergence of the Cauchy data on s, also if they are analytic, does in general not imply convergence of the corresponding solutions of the heat equation elsewhere (cf. the example given by PUCCI [59]). In the following we shall prove, however, that this convergence indeed occurs under the special circumstances of our approach.

If the data s, f (if $b>0$), g, and h in (13.20-24) are analytic and the inverse Stefan problem possesses a solution u^* (which can be guaranteed for $r = 1$ in case $b = 0$), then u^* can be expanded into a series of heat polynomials with powers $(t-t_0)^k$ which uniformly converges in a strip $-\infty < x < \infty$ and $|t-t_0| < \sigma$ where σ is the radius of convergence for the power series of s around t_0. (This can be concluded from Theorem 4.7 of COLTON [80]. For similar results see also WIDDER [75]). The following theorem now says that in this case the coefficients of the heat polynomials $\hat{u}_n$ of best approximation for the unconstrained defect minimization problem converge to the coefficients of the power series of u^*, which implies the uniform convergence of $\hat{u}_n$ to u^* in $\bar{\Omega}$.

The theorem is stated for the case $r = 1$. However, the reader may verify that it can be modified in order to hold true for $r>1$ as long as $\overline{\Omega(0)}$ is an r-dimensional simply connected region which contains the origin.

<u>Theorem 13.3.</u> Let $X_n = \langle v_0,\dots,v_n\rangle$, where v_i, $0 \le i \le n$, is the heat polynomial (12.13) defined on $\overline{D_T(s)}$, and let Assumption 13.5 be satisfied. Then if (13.20-24) has a unique solution $u^* \in C^{2,1}(\Omega) \cap C^{0,0}(\bar{\Omega})$, which can be expanded into a uniformly converging power series of heat polynomials on $\bar{\Omega}$, i.e. if u^* is such that there exist numbers $\hat{a}_i \in \mathbb{R}$ so that

$$\lim_{n\to\infty} \| u^* - \sum_{i=1}^{n} \hat{a}_i v_i \|_{\bar{\Omega}} = 0, \tag{13.29}$$

and if further $\hat{u}_n = \sum_{i=0}^{n} a_i^{(n)} v_i$ is a solution of the unconstrained minimization problem

$$(P_n') \quad \text{Minimize} \quad |||r - Tu|||_{\overline{\Omega(0)} \cup \bar{\Sigma}} \quad \text{on } X_n$$

($\hat{u}_n$ exists!), then we have

(1) $\lim_{n\to\infty} a_i^{(n)} = \hat{a}_i$ for each $i = 0,1,\ldots$

(2) $\lim_{n\to\infty} \| \frac{\partial^k}{\partial x^k} u^* - \frac{\partial^k}{\partial x^k} \hat{u}_n \|_{\bar{\Omega}} = 0$ for each $k = 0,1,\ldots$

<u>Proof.</u> We shall need Markov's inequality which provides that for each polynomial p_n of degree less than or equal to n

$$\max_{x\in[\alpha,\beta]} |p_n'(x)| \le n^2 \frac{2}{\beta-\alpha} \max_{x\in[\alpha,\beta]} |p_n(x)| \tag{13.30}$$

holds true (see CHENEY [66], p. 94).

Let us define now $R_n = \sum_{i=n+1}^{\infty} \hat{a}_i v_i$. Then due to the definition of $|||\cdot|||$ and the optimality of $\hat{u}_n$ we obtain

$$\|r_1 - \sum_{i=0}^{n} a_i^{(n)} v_i\|_{\overline{\Omega(0)}} \le |||r - T(\sum_{i=0}^{n} a_i^{(n)} v_i)|||_{\overline{\Omega(0)} \cup \bar{\Sigma}}$$

$$\le |||r - T(\sum_{i=0}^{n} \hat{a}_i v_i)|||_{\overline{\Omega(0)} \cup \bar{\Sigma}} = |||TR_n|||_{\overline{\Omega(0)} \cup \bar{\Sigma}} \tag{13.31}$$

where the right-hand side of (13.31) tends to zero because of (13.29) and because of

$$\lim_{n\to\infty} \| \frac{\partial^k}{\partial x^k} R_n \|_{\bar{\Omega}} = 0 \tag{13.32}$$

(see REEMTSEN/KIRSCH [84], p. 269). Thus, since r can be written in terms of the power series of u^* and since $v_0 = 1$ and $v_i(0,0) = 0, 1 \le i \le n$, for $(0,0) \in \overline{\Omega(0)}$, we arrive at

$$\lim_{n\to\infty} a_0^{(n)} = \hat{a}_0.$$

Next, using the fact that $v_i(x,0) = x^i$ and employing (13.30) and (13.31), we deduce

$$\|r_{1_x} - \sum_{i=0}^{n} a_i^{(n)} v_{i_x}\|_{\overline{\Omega(0)}} \le \|\sum_{i=0}^{n} (\hat{a}_i - a_i^{(n)}) v_{i_x}\|_{\overline{\Omega(0)}} + \|R_{n_x}\|_{\overline{\Omega(0)}}$$

$$\leq n^2 \frac{2}{b} \| \sum_{i=0}^{n} (\hat{a}_i - a_i^{(n)}) v_i \|_{\overline{\Omega(0)}} + \| R_{n_x} \|_{\overline{\Omega(0)}}$$

$$\leq n^2 \frac{4}{b} ||| TR_n |||_{\overline{\Omega(0)} \cup \bar{\Sigma}} + \| R_{n_x} \|_{\bar{\Omega}} . \qquad (13.33)$$

Since

$$n^2 \left| \frac{\partial^k}{\partial x^k} R_n(x,t) \right| \leq \sum_{i=n+1}^{\infty} i^2 \left| \hat{a}_i \frac{\partial^k}{\partial x^k} v_i(x,t) \right| ,$$

we can get similarly to (13.32)

$$\lim_{n \to \infty} n^2 \left\| \frac{\partial^k}{\partial x^k} R_n \right\|_{\bar{\Omega}} = 0. \qquad (13.34)$$

Hence, by (13.32) and (13.34) the right-hand side of (13.33) tends to zero such that using the identity $v_{i_x} = i\, v_{i-1}$ we obtain from (13.33)

$$\lim_{n \to \infty} a_i^{(n)} = \hat{a}_i \qquad (13.35)$$

for $i = 1$. It is now easily seen that we can similarly prove (13.35) for $i > 1$. Finally, statement (2) can be verified by simple arguments (cf. Theorem 3.1 in REEMTSEN/KIRSCH [84]). □

Appendix

14. STABILITY THEOREMS FOR THE CLASSICAL ONE-DIMENSIONAL STEFAN PROBLEM

Let $T > 0$, $b \geq 0$, β_1 and β_2 with $|\beta_1| + |\beta_2| > 0$ be given reals and let c and f be prescribed functions which will be specified later. Then we consider the following classical one-dimensional single-phase Stefan problem: find a couple of sufficiently smooth functions (u,s) such that

$$Lu(x,t) := u_{xx}(x,t) - u_t(x,t) = 0 \quad \text{in } D_T(s), \tag{14.1}$$

$$\beta_1 u(0,t) + \beta_2 u_x(0,t) = c(t), \quad 0 < t \leq T, \tag{14.2}$$

$$u(x,0) = f(x), \quad 0 \leq x \leq b, \tag{14.3}$$

$$u(s(t),t) = 0, \quad 0 < t \leq T, \tag{14.4}$$

$$u_x(s(t),t) = -\dot{s}(t), \quad 0 < t \leq T, \tag{14.5}$$

$$s(0) = b, \tag{14.6}$$

where for $s \in C[0,t]$ and $t \in [0,T]$

$$D_t(s) = \{(x,\tau) \in \mathbb{R}^2 \mid \; 0 < x < s(\tau), \; 0 < \tau \leq t\}.$$

In this section we want to derive computable bounds for the error between a solution (u,s) of (14.1-6) and an approximate solution $(\bar{u},\bar{s})$ of (u,s) which fulfills the differential equation (14.1) and the initial condition (14.6) but which does not satisfy (14.2-5) exactly. Hence there exist functions ρ_i, $i \in \{1,2,3,4\}$, such that $(\bar{u},\bar{s})$ is a solution of the perturbed problem

$$L\bar{u}(x,t) = 0 \quad \text{in } D_T(\bar{s}) \tag{14.7}$$

$$\beta_1 \bar{u}(0,t) + \beta_2 \bar{u}_x(0,t) = c(t) + \rho_1(t), \quad 0 < t \leq T, \tag{14.8}$$

$$\bar{u}(x,0) = f(x) + \rho_2(x), \quad 0 \leq x \leq b, \tag{14.9}$$

$$\bar{u}(\bar{s}(t),t) = \rho_3(t), \quad 0 < t \leq T, \tag{14.10}$$

$$u_x(\bar{s}(t),t) = -\dot{\bar{s}}(t) + \rho_4(t), \qquad 0 < t \le T, \tag{14.11}$$

$$\bar{s}(0) = b. \tag{14.12}$$

We assume that in case b = 0 the initial conditions (14.3) and (14.9) are omitted.

CANNON/HILL [67], CANNON/DOUGLAS [67], and CANNON/PRIMICERIO [71] showed that the problem (14.1-6) possesses a unique classical solution which depends continuously on the data if the data are sufficiently smooth and if either β_1 or β_2 vanishes. The results of these authors have been extended to more general Stefan problems by FASANO and PRIMICERIO [77a,b]. But while all of these authors were only concerned with the verification of stability, we want to use their ideas here in order to obtain computable stability estimates, i.e. computable error bounds for numerical schemes. Such bounds have also been given by KNABNER [83]. However, opposite to KNABNER and the other authors above we do not need to assume that the right-hand side of (14.10) equals zero, i.e. we can avoid the transformation $\bar{u} := \bar{u} - \rho_3$ which brings $\dot{\rho}_3$ into the differential equation (14.7) and thereby into the error bounds. (This means in particular that we can get around any extension of $\bar{u}$ outside of $\overline{D_T(\bar{s})}$). But let us mention that in contrast to KNABNER's bounds the size of the constants in our estimates is numerically acceptable only for small times.

We define now

$$\alpha(t) = \min(s(t),\bar{s}(t)), \quad \delta(t) = |s(t) - \bar{s}(t)|, \tag{14.13}$$

for $t \in [0,T]$ and

$$N = \|\dot{\bar{s}}\|_T \tag{14.14}$$

for $\bar{s} \in C^1[0,T]$ where

$$\|g\|_t = \max_{0 \le \tau \le t} |g(\tau)|, \quad g \in C[0,t].$$

Further we set

$$u(x,t) = 0 \quad \text{for } x > s(t) \text{ and } 0 \le t \le T. \tag{14.15}$$

Finally we point out that we will generally assume

$$\max\{\|\rho_1\|_T, \ \|\rho_2\|_b, \ \|\rho_3\|_T, \ \|\rho_4\|_T\} < 1.$$

This is reasonable since we are here not interested in reproving the continuous dependence of (u,s) on the data, but rather in obtaining error bounds for an approximate solution $(\bar{u},\bar{s})$ of (u,s). However, such a condition on the size of the errors is not needed for the temperature estimates below and could be avoided for the estimates of the free boundaries, however, for the price of a considerable increase of the bounds.

14.1. NEUMANN DATA

<u>Assumption 14.1.</u> Let $\beta_1 = 0$, $\beta_2 = 1$, and $b \geq 0$. Further, let $c \in C[0,T]$ and $c \leq 0$ in $[0,T]$, and in case $b > 0$ let $f \in C^1[0,b]$, $f \geq 0$ in $[0,b]$, $f'(0) = c(0)$, and $f(b) = 0$. In particular, if $b = 0$ let $c(0) < 0$.

CANNON and PRIMICERIO [71] proved that under Assumption 14.1 problem (14.1-6) possesses a unique solution $(u,s) \in C^{2,1}(D_T(s)) \cap C^{1,0}(\overline{D_T(s)}) \times C^1[0,T]$ (beside a possible discontinuity of u_x at (b,0) in case $b > 0$) which satisfies

$$0 \leq u(x,t) \leq H(t)(s(t) - x) \quad \text{in } \overline{D_T(s)}, \tag{14.16}$$

$$0 \leq \dot{s}(t) \leq H(t), \qquad 0 \leq t \leq T, \tag{14.17}$$

where

$$H(t) = \max\{\|c\|_t, \ \|f'\|_b\} \tag{14.18}$$

(see FRIEDMAN [59, 60] for the result $s \in C^1[0,T]$).

Let now $(\bar{u},\bar{s})$ be an approximate solution of (u,s) such that in addition to Assumption 14.1 the following assumption is fulfilled.

<u>Assumption 14.2.</u> For $\rho_2 \in C^1[0,b]$ (if $b > 0$) and $\rho_1, \rho_3, \rho_4 \in C[0,T]$ with

$$\varphi(t) = \max\{\|\rho_2\|_b, \ \|\rho_3\|_t\} < 1, \quad 0 \leq t \leq T, \tag{14.19}$$

let $(\bar{u},\bar{s}) \in C^{2,1}(D_T(\bar{s})) \cap C^{1,0}(\overline{D_T(\bar{s})}) \times C^1[0,T]$ be a solution of (14.7-12) where

$$\bar{s}(t) > 0 \quad \text{for} \quad 0 < t \leq T.$$

It is easily seen that all results of this subsection are valid for b = 0 if the terms containing f and ρ_2 are cancelled. Thus essentially we generalize here the bounds given by REEMTSEN and LOZANO [81] for the case b = 0. However, we want to point out that we were able to relax the assumptions on $\bar{s}$ here considerably which explains the slight modifications of the corresponding formulas of REEMTSEN and LOZANO [81] for b = 0.

<u>Lemma 14.1.</u> Under Assumptions 14.1 and 14.2 we have

$$- \varphi(t) - \|\rho_1\|_t(\|\bar{s}\|_t - x) \leq \bar{u}(x,t) \leq \varphi(t) + G(t)(\|\bar{s}\|_t - x) \tag{14.20}$$

in $\overline{D_T(\bar{s})}$ where

$$G(t) = \max\{\|c\|_t + \|\rho_1\|_t, \|f'\|_b\}. \tag{14.21}$$

<u>Proof.</u> We define

$$v(x,t) = \bar{u}(x,t) + \varphi(t_0) + \|\rho_1\|_{t_0}(\|\bar{s}\|_{t_0} - x)$$

in $\overline{D_{t_0}(\bar{s})}$ for $t_0 \in [0,T]$ and note that we have $\|\bar{s}\|_{t_0} \geq b$ by (14.12). Hence, recalling Assumption 14.1, we obtain

$$\begin{aligned}
&Lv(x,t) = 0 && \text{in } D_{t_0}(\bar{s}),\\
&v_x(0,t) = c(t) + \rho_1(t) - \|\rho_1\|_{t_0} \leq 0, && 0 < t \leq t_0,\\
&v(x,0) = f(x) + \rho_2(x) + \varphi(t_0) + \|\rho_1\|_{t_0}(\|\bar{s}\|_{t_0} - x) \geq 0, && 0 \leq x \leq b,\\
&v(\bar{s}(t),t) = \rho_3(t) + \varphi(t_0) + \|\rho_1\|_{t_0}(\|\bar{s}\|_{t_0} - \bar{s}(t)) \geq 0, && 0 < t \leq t_0.
\end{aligned}$$

By virtue of the weak maximum principle (see e.g. Lemma 18.1.2 by CANNON [84]), v has to be nonnegative in $\overline{D_{t_0}(\bar{s})}$ for each $t_0 \in [0,T]$. Thus the left inequality in (14.20) is verified.

Now we set

$$w(x,t) = \varphi(t_0) + G(t_0)(\|\bar{s}\|_{t_0} - x) - \bar{u}(x,t)$$

in $\overline{D_{t_0}(\bar{s})}$ and observe that

$$G(t)(\|\bar{s}\|_t - x) \geq H(t)(b-x) \geq f(x) - f(b) = f(x).$$

Then we have

$$Lw(x,t) = 0 \qquad \text{in } D_{t_0}(\bar{s}),$$

$$w_x(0,t) = -G(t_0) - c(t) - \rho_1(t) \leq 0, \qquad 0 < t \leq t_0,$$

$$w(x,0) = \varphi(t_0) + G(t_0)(\|\bar{s}\|_{t_0} - x) - f(x) - \rho_2(x) \geq 0, \quad 0 \leq x \leq b,$$

$$w(\bar{s}(t),t) = \varphi(t_0) + G(t_0)(\|\bar{s}\|_{t_0} - \bar{s}(t)) - \rho_3(t) \geq 0, \quad 0 < t \leq t_0.$$

Consequently w is nonnegative in $\overline{D_{t_0}(\bar{s})}$ for each $t_0 \in [0,T]$, and everything is proved. □

We continue by deriving a bound for $|u-\bar{u}|$ in $\overline{D_T(\bar{s})}$.

<u>Theorem 14.1.</u> Let Assumptions 14.1 and 14.2 be fulfilled. Then

$$|(u-\bar{u})(x,t)| \leq \varphi(t) + G(t)\|s-\bar{s}\|_t + \|\rho_1\|_t(\|\bar{s}\|_t - x) \quad \text{in } \overline{D_T(\bar{s})}$$

where G is defined by (14.21).

<u>Proof.</u> Due to (14.17) we have $s(t) = \|s\|_t$. Hence employing (14.4), (14.10), (14.16), and (14.19), we can get the following estimation:

$$\begin{aligned} |(u-\bar{u})(\alpha(t),t)| &\leq |u(\alpha(t),t)| + |\bar{u}(\alpha(t),t)| \\ &\leq \begin{Bmatrix} H(t)\delta(t) + |\rho_3(t)| & \text{if } \alpha(t) = \bar{s}(t) \\ \varphi(t) + G(t)(\|\bar{s}\|_t - s(t)) & \text{if } \alpha(t) = s(t) \end{Bmatrix} \\ &\leq \varphi(t) + G(t)\|\delta\|_t. \end{aligned}$$

Thus if

$$z(x,t) = \varphi(t_0) + G(t_0)\|\delta\|_{t_0} + \|\rho_1\|_{t_0}(\|\alpha\|_{t_0} - x) \pm (u(x,t) - \bar{u}(x,t))$$

in $\overline{D_{t_0}(\alpha)}$ for $t_0 \in [0,T]$, we arrive at

$$\begin{aligned}
&Lz(x,t) = 0 && \text{in } D_{t_0}(\alpha),\\
&z_x(0,t) = -\|\rho_1\|_{t_0} \mp \rho_1(t) \le 0, && 0 < t \le t_0,\\
&z(x,0) = \varphi(t_0) + G(t_0)\|\delta\|_{t_0} + \|\rho_1\|_{t_0}(\|\alpha\|_{t_0} - x) \mp \rho_2(x) \ge 0, && 0 \le x \le b,\\
&z(\alpha(t),t) = \varphi(t_0) + G(t_0)\|\delta\|_{t_0} + \|\rho_1\|_{t_0}(\|\alpha\|_{t_0} - \alpha(t)) &&\\
&\qquad \pm (u(\alpha(t),t) - \bar{u}(\alpha(t),t)) \ge 0, && 0 < t \le t_0.
\end{aligned}$$

Therefore, z is nonnegative in $\overline{D_T(\alpha)}$. At last we deduce from (14.15) and (14.20) that for all (x,t) with $s(t) \le x \le \bar{s}(t)$ and $0 \le t \le T$

$$|(u-\bar{u})(x,t)| = |\bar{u}(x,t)| \le \varphi(t) + G(t)(\|\bar{s}\|_t - x) \le \varphi(t) + G(t)\|\delta\|_t. \qquad \square$$

A bound for $\|s-\bar{s}\|_t$ is determined by the following theorem.

<u>Theorem 14.2.</u> Let Assumptions 14.1 and 14.2 be satisfied and let $M = \max(N, H(T))$ with N and $H(T)$ defined by (14.14) and (14.18). Further, let $\|\rho_1\|_T$ be sufficiently small such that in addition to (14.19)

$$\mu(t) = \varphi(t) + \|\rho_1\|_t\,(b + NT) < 1$$

holds true. Then we have

$$\|s-\bar{s}\|_t \le A(t)[1 + 2C(t)t^{1/2}]\exp(\pi C(t)^2 t)$$

with

$$A(t) = R(t)[(2\|\rho_1\|_t + \|\rho_3\|_t\,N + \|\rho_4\|_t)t + 2b\|\rho_2\|_b + 2\pi^{-1/2}Q(t)\varphi(t)t^{1/2}]$$

and

$$C(t) = \pi^{-1/2} Q(t) G(t) R(t)$$

where G is defined by (14.21),

$$R(t) = 1/(1-\mu(t)), \text{ and } Q(t) = [1+\pi^{-1/2} M t^{1/2}]\exp(M^2 t/4). \tag{14.22}$$

Proof. We first note that in case $\bar{s}(t) > s(t)$ for $t \in [0,T]$, Lemma 14.1 implies

$$-\int_{s(t)}^{\bar{s}(t)} \bar{u}(x,t)dx \le [\varphi(t) + \|\rho_1\|_t \|\bar{s}\|_t]\delta(t) \le [\varphi(t) + \|\rho_1\|_t (b+NT)]\delta(t).$$

Hence following the proof of Lemma 2 of REEMTSEN and LOZANO [81] we can obtain here

$$\delta(t) \le R(t)\{|k(t)| + |\int_0^{\alpha(t)} (u(x,t) - \bar{u}(x,t))dx|\} \tag{14.23}$$

with R(t) (14.22) and

$$k(t) = \int_0^t (\rho_4(\tau) - \rho_1(\tau) + \rho_3(\tau)\dot{\bar{s}}(\tau))d\tau + \int_0^b \rho_2(x)dx.$$

In order to estimate now the integral in (14.23), we write $\bar{u}(x,t) - u(x,t) = v_1(x,t) + v_2(x,t) + v_3(x,t)$ where the v_i, $i \in \{1,2,3\}$, satisfy $Lv_i = 0$ in $D_T(\alpha)$ and

$$\begin{array}{lll} v_{1_x}(0,t) = \rho_1(t), & v_{2_x}(0,t) = 0, & v_{3_x}(0,t) = 0, \\ v_1(x,0) = 0, & v_2(x,0) = 0, & v_3(x,0) = \rho_2(x), \\ v_1(\alpha(t),t) = 0, & v_2(\alpha(t),t) = (\bar{u}-u)(\alpha(t),t), & v_3(\alpha(t),t) = 0, \end{array}$$

for $0 < t \le T$ and $0 \le x \le b$. Then we have

$$|\int_0^{\alpha(t)} v_1(x,t)dx| \le \int_0^t |\rho_1(\tau)|d\tau \text{ and } |\int_0^{\alpha(t)} v_3(x,t)dx| \le \int_0^b |\rho_2(x)|dx \tag{14.24}$$

(cf. CANNON/DOUGLAS [67], p. 86-87). Further, observing that

$$|\alpha(t) - \alpha(\tau)| \le M\ |t-\tau| \quad \text{for all } t,\tau \in [0,T]$$

for $M = \max(N,H(T))$, we can follow the proof of Lemma 4 of REEMTSEN and LOZANO [81] and deduce

$$\left|\int_0^{\alpha(t)} v_2(x,t)dx\right| \le \frac{\varphi(t)Q(t)}{\pi^{1/2}}\int_0^t (t-\tau)^{-1/2}d\tau + \frac{G(t)Q(t)}{\pi^{1/2}}\int_0^t \frac{\|\delta\|_\tau d\tau}{(t-\tau)^{1/2}} \tag{14.25}$$

where G and Q are defined by (14.21) and (14.22).

Thus, δ (14.23) can be estimated by (14.24) and (14.25). Finally, the Gronwall type Lemma 5 in REEMTSEN and LOZANO [81] (a modification of Lemma 2 of CANNON [64]) can be applied to this estimation, and the proof is complete. □

14.2. DIRICHLET DATA

14.2.1. THE CASE $b > 0$

Assumption 14.3. Let $\beta_1 = 1$, $\beta_2 = 0$, and $b > 0$. Further, let $c \in C[0,T]$ with $c \ge 0$ in $[0,T]$ and $f \in C^1[0,b]$ with $f \ge 0$ in $[0,b]$, $c(0) = f(0)$ and $f(b) = 0$ be given.

Under Assumption 14.3 problem (14.1-6) possesses a unique solution $(u,s) \in C^{2,1}(D_T(s)) \cap C^{0,0}(\overline{D_T(s)}) \times C^1[0,T]$ which satisfies

$$0 \le u(x,t) \le M(t)(s(t)-x) \quad \text{in } \overline{D_T(s)}, \tag{14.26}$$

$$0 \le \dot{s}(t) \le M(t), \qquad 0 \le t \le T, \tag{14.27}$$

where

$$M(t) = \max\{b^{-1}\|c\|_t, \|f'\|_b\} \tag{14.28}$$

(see CANNON/HILL [67] and FRIEDMAN [59]). Let now $(\bar{u},\bar{s})$ be an approximate solution of (u,s) which fulfills the following assumption.

Assumption 14.4. Let $\rho_2 \in C^1[0,b]$ and $\rho_1, \rho_3, \rho_4 \in C[0,T]$ be such that

$$\xi(t) = \max\{\|\rho_1\|_t, \|\rho_2\|_b, \|\rho_3\|_t\} < 1 \tag{14.29}$$

for $0 \le t \le T$. Further, let $(\bar{u},\bar{s}) \in C^{2,1}(D_T(\bar{s})) \cap C^{0,0}(\overline{D_T(\bar{s})}) \times C^1[0,T]$ be a solution of (14.7-12) with

$$\bar{s}(t) > b \quad \text{for} \quad 0 < t \le T. \tag{14.30}$$

We note that in comparison with (14.27) we require for $\bar{s}$ only the relatively weak condition (14.30).

Again, we first provide now a bound on $\bar{u}$ in $\overline{D_T(\bar{s})}$ which corresponds to the bound (14.26) on u in $\overline{D_T(s)}$.

Lemma 14.2. Under Assumptions 14.3 and 14.4

$$-\xi(t) \le \bar{u}(x,t) \le \xi(t) + M(t)(\|\bar{s}\|_t - x) \quad \text{in } \overline{D_T(\bar{s})} \tag{14.31}$$

is true where M and ξ are defined by (14.28) and (14.29).

Proof. The first inequality in (14.31) follows from equations (14.7-10) by virtue of the maximum principle (see e.g. Theorem 1.6.1 of CANNON [84]) and Assumption 14.3. The second inequality in (14.31) can be proved similarly to the second inequality in (14.20). □

Moreover, bounds for $|u-\bar{u}|$ in $\overline{D_T(\bar{s})}$ and $\|s-\bar{s}\|_t$ are given by the following two theorems.

Theorem 14.3. Under Assumptions 14.3 and 14.4 we have with M (14.28) and ξ (14.29)

$$|(u-\bar{u})(x,t)| \le \xi(t) + M(t) \ \|s-\bar{s}\|_t \quad \text{in } \overline{D_T(\bar{s})}. \tag{14.32}$$

Proof. From (14.4), (14.10), (14.28), and (14.31) we can easily conclude that with α (14.13)

$$|(u-\bar{u})(\alpha(t),t)| \le \xi(t) + M(t) \ \|s-\bar{s}\|_t, \quad 0 \le t \le T. \tag{14.33}$$

Using similar arguments as in the proof of Theorem 14.1, we can next show that

$$z(x,t) = \xi(t) + M(t) \ \|s-\bar{s}\|_t \pm (u(x,t) - \bar{u}(x,t))$$

is nonnegative in $\overline{D_T(\alpha)}$. Finally, for all (x,t) with $s(t) \le x \le \bar{s}(t)$ and $0 \le t \le T$, (14.32) is true because of (14.15) and (14.31). □

Theorem 14.4. Let Assumptions 14.3 and 14.4 be fulfilled and $C = \max(N, M(T))$ with N and M defined by (14.14) and (14.28). Then we have

$$\|s-\bar{s}\|_t \le X(t)[1+2Y(t)t^{1/2}]\exp(\pi Y(t)^2 t)$$

where X and Y are defined by

$$X(t) = \frac{1}{b(1-\xi(t))}[2t\|\rho_1\|_t + (\frac{1}{2}N^2 t + bN + 1)t\|\rho_3\|_t + (Nt+b)t\|\rho_4\|_t + b^2\|\rho_2\|_b + 2\xi(t)Z(t)t^{1/2}] \tag{14.34}$$

and

$$Y(t) = \frac{1}{b(1-\xi(t))} M(t)Z(t) \tag{14.35}$$

with ξ (14.29),

$$Z(t) = 4(Ct+b)\pi^{-1/2}[1+2A(t)t^{1/2}]\exp(\pi A(t)^2 t) \tag{14.36}$$

and

$$A(t) = \pi^{-1/2}\left(\frac{1}{b}+\frac{C}{2}\right). \tag{14.37}$$

Proof. Applying Stoke's theorem, we can obtain for $0 \le t \le T$

$$s(t)^2 = b^2 + 2\int_0^t c(\tau)d\tau - 2\int_0^{s(t)} xu(x,t)dx + 2\int_0^b xf(x)dx \tag{14.38}$$

(see CANNON/HILL [67]). The corresponding equation for $\bar{s}$ is

$$\bar{s}(t)^2 = b^2 + 2\int_0^t c(\tau)d\tau - 2\int_0^{\bar{s}(t)} x\bar{u}(x,t)dx + 2\int_0^b xf(x)dx + 2q(t) \tag{14.39}$$

where

$$q(t) = \int_0^b x\rho_2(x)dx + \int_0^t[\bar{s}(\tau)\dot{\bar{s}}(\tau)\rho_3(\tau)+\bar{s}(\tau)\rho_4(\tau)-\rho_3(\tau)+\rho_1(\tau)]d\tau. \tag{14.40}$$

Next, we observe that due to (14.6), (14.27), and (14.30)

$$|s(t)-\bar{s}(t)| = \frac{|s(t)^2-\bar{s}(t)^2|}{|s(t)+\bar{s}(t)|} \le \frac{|s(t)^2-\bar{s}(t)^2|}{2b}. \tag{14.41}$$

Let now first $s(t) \ge \bar{s}(t)$. Then employing (14.38), (14.39), and (14.41), we arrive at

$$\begin{aligned} 0 \le s(t)-\bar{s}(t) &\le \frac{1}{b}\Big[\int_0^{\bar{s}(t)} x\bar{u}(x,t)dx - \int_0^{s(t)} xu(x,t)dx - q(t)\Big] \\ &\le \frac{1}{b}\Big[\int_0^{\bar{s}(t)} x(\bar{u}(x,t)-u(x,t))dx - q(t)\Big] \end{aligned} \tag{14.42}$$

where we used the nonnegativity of u in $\overline{D_T(s)}$. On the other hand, if $\bar{s}(t) > s(t)$, we conclude from (14.31), (14.38), (14.39), and (14.41) that

$$\begin{aligned} 0 \le \bar{s}(t)-s(t) &\le \frac{\bar{s}(t)^2-s(t)^2}{2b} = \frac{1}{b}\Big[\int_0^{s(t)} x(u(x,t)-\bar{u}(x,t))dx \\ &\quad - \int_{s(t)}^{\bar{s}(t)} x\bar{u}(x,t)dx + q(t)\Big] \\ &\le \frac{1}{b}\Big[\int_0^{s(t)} x(u(x,t)-\bar{u}(x,t))dx + \xi(t)\frac{\bar{s}(t)^2-s(t)^2}{2} + q(t)\Big]. \end{aligned}$$

Hence, due to (14.29) we have

$$\begin{aligned} 0 \le \bar{s}(t)-s(t) &\le \frac{\bar{s}(t)^2-s(t)^2}{2b} \\ &\le \frac{1}{b(1-\xi(t))}\Big[\int_0^{s(t)} x(u(x,t)-\bar{u}(x,t))dx + q(t)\Big]. \end{aligned} \tag{14.43}$$

Combination of (14.42) and (14.43) finally yields

$$\delta(t) \le \frac{1}{b(1-\xi(t))}\Big[\Big|\int_0^{\alpha(t)} x(u(x,t)-\bar{u}(x,t))dx\Big| + |q(t)|\Big]. \tag{14.44}$$

We remark that (14.44) does not contain any integral with the bounds $\min(s(t), \bar{s}(t))$ and $\max(s(t), \bar{s}(t))$, in contrast to the corresponding inequality in CANNON and HILL [67]. By this means we can avoid estimating $\bar{u}$ outside of $\overline{D_T(\bar{s})}$.

In order to obtain now a bound on the integral in (14.44), we make use of ideas of CANNON and HILL [67].

Because of (14.33), $|u - \bar{u}|$ is dominated in $\overline{D_T(\alpha)}$ by $v + w$ where v and w are solutions of

$$Lv(x,t) = 0, \quad 0 < x < \infty, \quad 0 < t \le T,$$

$$v(0,t) = |\rho_1(t)|, \quad 0 < t \le T,$$

$$v(x,0) = \begin{cases} |\rho_2(x)|, & 0 \le x \le b, \\ 0, & b < x < \infty, \end{cases}$$

and

$$Lw(x,t) = 0, \quad 0 < x < \alpha(t), \quad 0 < t \le T,$$

$$w(0,t) = 0, \quad 0 < t \le T,$$

$$w(x,0) = 0, \quad 0 \le x \le b,$$

$$w(\alpha(t),t) = \xi(t) + M(t)\|\delta\|_t, \quad 0 < t \le T.$$

For v we can obtain the following estimation

$$\left| \int_0^{\alpha(t)} xv(x,t)dx \right| \le \int_0^t |\rho_1(\tau)|d\tau + \int_0^b x|\rho_2(x)|dx \tag{14.45}$$

(see CANNON and HILL [67], p. 9). Next, w can be written as

$$w(x,t) = \int_0^t \sigma(\tau)[K_x(x,t,-\alpha(\tau),\tau) + K_x(x,t,\alpha(\tau),\tau)]d\tau$$

where

$$K(x,t,\xi,\tau) = \frac{1}{2\pi^{1/2}(t-\tau)^{1/2}} \exp\{-\frac{(x-\xi)^2}{4(t-\tau)}\} \tag{14.46}$$

and σ is a solution of

$$\sigma(t) = 2(\xi(t) + M(t)\|\delta\|_t) - 2\int_0^t \sigma(\tau)[K_x(\alpha(t),t-\alpha(\tau),\tau) + K_x(\alpha(t),t,\alpha(\tau),\tau)]d\tau. \tag{14.47}$$

We observe that α is Lipschitz bounded with constant $C = \max(N, M(T))$ where N and $M(T)$ are given by (14.14) and (14.28). Hence, for $0 < \tau \le t$ we have

$$\frac{\alpha(t)+\alpha(\tau)}{2(t-\tau)} \exp\{-\frac{(\alpha(t)+\alpha(\tau))^2}{4(t-\tau)}\} \le \frac{2}{\alpha(t)+\alpha(\tau)} \le \frac{1}{b}$$

and, therefore, from (14.47)

$$|\sigma(t)| \le 2[\xi(t) + M(t)\|\delta\|_t] + A(t) \int_0^t \frac{|\sigma(\tau)|}{(t-\tau)^{1/2}} d\tau \tag{14.48}$$

with A(t) (14.37). Applying now Lemma 5 of REEMTSEN and LOZANO [81] to (14.48), we arrive at

$$|\sigma(t)| \le 2[\xi(t) + M(t)\|\delta\|_t][1 + 2A(t)t^{1/2}]\exp(\pi A(t)^2 t). \tag{14.49}$$

Hence, with Z(t) (14.36) we establish

$$\int_0^{\alpha(t)} xw(x,t)dx \le \int_0^t |\sigma(\tau)|\alpha(t) \frac{4}{2\pi^{1/2}(t-\tau)^{1/2}} d\tau$$

$$\le \frac{2(Ct+b)}{\pi^{1/2}} \int_0^t \frac{|\sigma(\tau)|d\tau}{(t-\tau)^{1/2}} \le 2\xi(t)Z(t)t^{1/2} + M(t)Z(t) \int_0^t \frac{\|\delta\|_\tau d\tau}{(t-\tau)^{1/2}} \tag{14.50}$$

(see CANNON/HILL [67], p. 10).

Employing finally (14.40), (14.45), and (14.50), we can estimate (14.44) by

$$\delta(t) \le X(t) + Y(t) \int_0^t \frac{\|\delta\|_\tau d\tau}{(t-\tau)^{1/2}}$$

where X(t) and Y(t) are defined by (14.34) and (14.35). Another application of Lemma 5 by REEMTSEN and LOZANO [81] finishes the proof. □

14.2.2. THE CASE b = 0.

Assumption 14.5. Let $\beta_1 = 1$, $\beta_2 = 0$, and $b = 0$. Let further $c \in C[0,T]$ satisfy

$$lt \le c(t) \le Lt \quad \text{for} \quad 0 \le t \le T$$

with positive constants l and L.

From CANNON/HILL [67] we get that under Assumption 14.5 problem (14.1-6) has a unique solution $(u,s) \in C^{2,1}(D_T(s)) \cap C^{0,0}(\overline{D_T(s)}) \times C^1(0,T]$ with the following properties

$$0 \le u(x,t) \le L\lambda^{-1}(s(t) - x) \quad \text{in } \overline{D_T(s)},$$
$$\lambda t \le s(t) \le L\lambda^{-1}t, \qquad 0 \le t \le T,$$
$$0 \le \dot{s}(t) \le L\lambda^{-1}, \qquad 0 \le t \le T,$$

where

$$\lambda = [T^{-1} \log(1 + lT)]^{1/2}.$$

In addition to Assumption 14.5 we further assume the following.

<u>Assumption 14.6.</u> Let $\rho_1, \rho_3, \rho_4 \in C[0,T]$ and let

$$\xi(t) = \max\{\|\rho_1\|_t, \|\rho_3\|_t\} < 1 \tag{14.51}$$

for $0 \le t \le T$. Further, let $(\bar{u},\bar{s}) \in C^{2,1}(D_T(\bar{s})) \cap C^{0,0}(\overline{D_T(\bar{s})}) \times C^1[0,T]$ be a solution of (14.7-12) for which

$$\bar{s}(t) \ge \lambda t \quad \text{for} \quad 0 \le t \le T.$$

Lemma 14.2 and Theorem 14.3 remain true for b = 0 if Assumptions 14.3 and 14.4 are replaced by Assumptions 14.5 and 14.6, and if $\xi(t)$ (14.51) and $M(t) = L\lambda^{-1}$ are chosen. We conclude this section by deriving a bound for $\|s-\bar{s}\|_t$ in case b = 0.

<u>Theorem 14.5.</u> If Assumptions 14.5 and 14.6 are fulfilled and if we set $C = \max(N, L\lambda^{-1})$ with N (14.14), then we have

$$\|s-\bar{s}\|_t \le I(t)[1 + 2V(t)t^{1/2}]\exp(\pi V(t)^2 t)$$

with

$$I(t) = \frac{1}{\lambda(1-\xi(t))} [2\|\rho_1\|_t + (\frac{N^2}{2}t + 1)\|\rho_3\|_t + Nt\|\rho_4\|_t + \frac{4C\xi(t)W(t)t^{1/2}}{\pi^{1/2}}] \tag{14.52}$$

and

$$V(t) = \frac{1}{\lambda(1-\xi(t))} [\frac{2CL\lambda^{-1}W(t)}{\pi^{1/2}}] \tag{14.53}$$

where

$$W(t) = (1 + \frac{C}{\pi^{1/2}} t^{1/2})\exp(\frac{C^2}{4} t) \tag{14.54}$$

and $\xi(t)$ is defined by (14.51).

<u>Proof.</u> Setting b = 0 and observing that $s(t) + \bar{s}(t) \geq 2\lambda t$, we can derive similarly to (14.44)

$$\delta(t) \leq \frac{1}{\lambda t(1-\xi(t))} [|\int_0^{\alpha(t)} x(u(x,t)-\bar{u}(x,t))dx| + |q(t)|] \tag{14.55}$$

with q(t) (14.40). Furthermore, in $\overline{D_T(\alpha)}$ $|u-\bar{u}|$ is dominated by v + w where v and w are solutions of

$$Lv(x,t) = 0, \quad 0 < x < \infty, \quad 0 < t \leq T,$$

$$v(0,t) = |\rho_1(t)|, \quad 0 < t \leq T,$$

$$v(x,0) = 0, \quad 0 \leq x < \infty,$$

and

$$Lw(x,t) = 0, \quad -\infty < x < \alpha(t), \quad 0 < t \leq T,$$

$$w(x,0) = 0, \quad -\infty < x < 0,$$

$$w(\alpha(t),t) = \xi(t) + L\lambda^{-1}\|\delta\|_t, \quad 0 < t \leq T.$$

Then recalling (14.45) we obtain

$$|\int_0^{\alpha(t)} xv(x,t)dx| \leq \int_0^t |\rho_1(\tau)|d\tau. \tag{14.56}$$

Now w can be written as

$$w(x,t) = \int_0^t \zeta(\tau)K_x(x,t,\alpha(\tau),\tau)d\tau, \quad x<\alpha(t),$$

with K (14.46) and ζ being solution of

$$\zeta(t) = 2(\xi(t) + L\lambda^{-1}\|\delta\|_t) - 2\int_0^t \zeta(\tau)K_x(\alpha(t),t,\alpha(\tau),\tau)d\tau.$$

If $|\zeta(t)|$ is estimated in the usual fashion, we arrive at

$$|\zeta(t)| \le 2[\xi(t) + L\lambda^{-1}\|\delta\|_t]W(t)$$

where W is given by (14.54). Thus we obtain

$$\begin{aligned}\int_0^{\alpha(t)} xw(x,t)dx &= \int_0^t \zeta(\tau)\{\int_0^{\alpha(t)} x K_x(x,t,\alpha(\tau),\tau)dx\}d\tau \\ &= \int_0^t \zeta(\tau)\{\alpha(t)K(\alpha(t),t,\alpha(\tau),\tau) - \int_0^{\alpha(t)} K(x,t,\alpha(\tau),\tau)dx\}d\tau \\ &\le \int_0^t |\zeta(\tau)|\alpha(t)\frac{2}{2\pi^{1/2}(t-\tau)^{1/2}}d\tau \\ &\le \frac{4C\xi(t)W(t)t^{3/2}}{\pi^{1/2}} + \frac{2CL\lambda^{-1}W(t)t}{\pi^{1/2}}\int_0^t \frac{\|\delta\|_\tau}{(t-\tau)^{1/2}}d\tau. \qquad (14.57)\end{aligned}$$

Finally, from (14.55), (14.56), and (14.57) we conclude that

$$\delta(t) \le I(t) + V(t)\int_0^t \frac{\|\delta\|_\tau}{(t-\tau)^{1/2}}d\tau$$

where I and V are defined by (14.52) and (14.53). Another application of Lemma 5 by REEMTSEN and LOZANO [81] yields the requested result. □

References

ALLINGER, G. and HENRY, M. [76]: Approximate solutions of differential equations with deviating arguments. SIAM J. Numer. Anal. 13 (1976), 412 - 426

ATKINSON, K.E. [76]: A survey of numerical methods for the solution of Fredholm integral equations of the second kind. Society for Industrial and Applied Mathematics, Philadelphia, Pennsylvania, 1976.

BACOPOULOS, A. and KARTSATOS, A.G. [72]: On polynomials approximating the solutions of nonlinear differential equations. Pacific J. Math. 40 (1972), 1 - 5.

BARRODALE, I. and YOUNG, A. [70]: Computational experience in solving linear operator equations using the Chebyshew norm. In "Numerical approximations to functions and data" (J.G. Hayes, Ed.), pp. 115 - 142, The Athlone Press, London, 1970.

BAUMEISTER, H., HOFFMANN, K.-H. and JOCHUM, P. [80]: Numerical solution of a parabolic free boundary value problem via Newton's method. J. Inst. Math. Applics. 25 (1980), 99 - 109.

BERNFELD, S. and LAKSHMIKANTHAM, V. [74]: An introduction to nonlinear boundary value problems. Academic Press, Inc., New York/London, 1974.

BOGAR, G. and JEPPSON, R. [80]: Approximate solutions of linear differential systems with boundary conditions. In "Approximation Theory III" (E.W. Cheney, Ed.), pp. 233 - 236, Academic Press, New York/London, 1980.

BRAESS, D. [73]: Chebyshev approximation by exponentials on finite subsets. Math. Comp. 27 (1973), 327 - 331.

BURKE, M.E. [76]: Nonlinear best approximations on discrete sets. J. Approx. Theory 16 (1976), 133 - 141.

CANNON, J.R. [64]: A priori estimate for continuation of the solution of the heat equation in the space variable. Ann. Math. Pura Appl. 65 (1964), 377 - 387.

CANNON, J.R. [84]: The one-dimensional heat equation. Addison-Wesley, Menlo Park, California, 1984.

CANNON, J.R. and DOUGLAS, J. [67]: The stability of the free boundary in a Stefan problem. Ann. Scuola Norm. Sup. Pisa 21 (1967), 83 - 91.

CANNON, J.R. and DOUGLAS, J. [67a]: The Cauchy problem for the heat equation. SIAM J. Numer. Anal. 4 (1967), 317 - 336.

CANNON, J.R. and HILL, C.D. [67]: Existence, uniqueness, stability and monotone dependence in a Stefan problem for the heat equation. J. Math. Mech. 17 (1967), 1 - 19.

CANNON, J.R. and PRIMICERIO, M. [71]: Remarks on the one-phase Stefan problem for the heat equation with flux prescribed on the fixed boundary. J. Math. Anal. Appl. 35 (1971), 361 - 373.

CHALMERS, B.A. [78]: On the rate of convergence of discretization in Chebyshev approximation. SIAM J. Numer. Anal. 15 (1978), 612 - 617.

CHENEY, E.W. [66]: Introduction to approximation theory. McGraw-Hill, New York, 1966.

CHEUNG, T.-Y. [78]: Recent developments in the numerical solution of partial differential equations by linear programming. SIAM Review 20 (1978), 139 - 167.

COLLATZ, L. [52]: Aufgaben monotoner Art. Archiv der Mathematik 3 (1952), 366 - 376.

COLLATZ, L. [59]: Approximation in partial differential equations. In "On numerical approximation" (R.E. Langer, Ed.), pp. 413 - 422, The University of Wisconsin Press, Madison, 1959.

COLLATZ, L. [66]: Functional analysis and numerical mathematics. Academic Press, New York/London, 1966.

COLLATZ, L. [80]: Anwendung von Monotoniesätzen zur Einschließung der Lösungen von Gleichungen. Inst. f. Angew. Mathematik, Univ. Hamburg, Preprint 80/15, 1980.

COLLATZ, L., GÜNTHER, H., and SPREKELS, J. [76]: Vergleich zwischen Diskretisierungsverfahren und parametrischen Methoden an einfachen Beispielen. ZAMM 56 (1976), 1 - 11.

COLLATZ, L. and KRABS, W. [73]: Approximationstheorie. Teubner, Stuttgart, 1973.

COLTON, D. [74]: The inverse Stefan problem for the heat equation in two space variables. Mathematika 21 (1974), 282 - 286.

COLTON, D.L. [80]: Analytic theory of partial differential equations. Pitman, Boston/London/Melbourne, 1980.

COLTON, D. and REEMTSEN, R. [84]: The numerical solution of the inverse Stefan problem in two space variables. SIAM J. Appl. Math. 44 (1984), 996 - 1013.

DAVIS, P.J. [75]: Interpolation and approximation. Dover Publications, New York, 1975.

DEM'YANOV, V.F. and MALOZEMOV, V.N. [74]: Introduction to minimax. John Wiley & Sons, New York/Toronto, 1974.

DUNHAM, C.B. [72]: Minimax nonlinear approximation by approximation on subsets. Comm. A.C.M. 15 (1972), 351.

FASANO, A. and PRIMICERIO, M. [77a]: General free boundary problems for the heat equation, I. J. Math. Anal. Appl. 57 (1977), 694 - 723.

FASANO, A. and PRIMICERIO, M. [77b]: General free boundary problems for the heat equation, II. J. Math. Anal. Appl. 58 (1977), 202 - 231.

FASANO, A. and PRIMICERIO, M. [77c]: General free boundary problems for the heat equation, III. J. Math. Anal. Appl. 59 (1977), 1 - 14.

FISHER, S.D. and JEROME, J.W. [75]: Minimum norm extremals in function spaces. Springer-Verlag, Berlin/Heidelberg/New York, 1975.

FRIEDMAN, A. [59]: Free boundary problems for parabolic equations I. Melting of solids. J. Math. Mech. 8 (1959), 499 - 517.

FRIEDMAN, A. [60]: Remarks on Stefan type free boundary problems for parabolic equations. J. Math. Mech. 9 (1960), 885 - 903.

FURZELAND, R.M. [80]: A comparative study of numerical methods for moving boundary problems. J. Inst. Maths. Applics. 26 (1980), 411 - 429.

GEVREY, M. [13]: Sur les équations aux dérivées partielles du type parabolique. J. Math. Ser. (6) 9 (1913), 305 - 471.

GROTHKOPF, U. [81]: Anwendungen nichtlinearer Optimierung auf Randwertaufgaben bei partiellen Differentialgleichungen. In "Numerische Behandlung von Differentialgleichungen, Band 3" (J. Albrecht, L. Collatz, Eds.), ISNM 56, pp. 73 - 82, Birkhäuser Verlag, Basel/Boston/Stuttgart, 1981.

HENRY, M.S. [69]: A best approximate solution of certain nonlinear differential equations, SIAM J. Numer. Anal. 6 (1969), 143 - 148.

HENRY, M.S. [70]: Best approximate solutions of nonlinear differential equations. J. Approx. Theory 3 (1970), 59 - 65.

HENRY, M.S. [73]: Best approximate solutions on finite point sets of nonlinear differential equations. J. Approx. Theory 7 (1973), 256 - 264.

HENRY, M.S. and WIGGINS, K.L. [76]: Applications of approximation theory to the initial value problem. J. Approx. Theory 17 (1976), 66 - 85.

HENRY, M.S. and WIGGINS, K.L. [78]: Applications of approximation theory to differential equations with deviating arguments. Pacific J. Math. 76 (1978), 431 - 441.

HENRY, M.S. and WIGGINS, K. [81]: Approximation theory methods for linear and nonlinear differential equations with deviating arguments. SIAM J. Math. Anal. 12 (1981), 342 - 354.

HERRERA, I. [84]: Boundary methods: an algebraic theory. Pitman, Boston/London/Melbourne, 1984.

HETTICH, R. and ZENCKE, P. [82]: Numerische Methoden der Approximation und semi-infiniten Optimierung. Teubner, Stuttgart, 1982.

HILL, C.D. [67]: Parabolic equations in one space variable and the non-characteristic Cauchy problem. Comm. Pure Appl. Math. 20 (1967), 619 - 633.

HUFFSTUTTLER, R.G. and STEIN, F.M. [68a]: The approximate solution of certain nonlinear differential equations. Proc. Amer. Math. Soc. 19 (1968), 998 - 1002.

HUFFSTUTTLER, R.G. and STEIN, F.M. [68b]: The approximate solution of y' = F(x,y). Pacific J. Math. 24 (1968), 283 - 289.

JOCHUM, P. [78]: Optimale Kontrolle von Stefan-Problemen mit Methoden der nichtlinearen Approximationstheorie. Dissertation, Ludwig-Maximilians-Universität, München, 1978.

JOCHUM, P. [80]: The inverse Stefan problem as a problem of nonlinear approximation theory. J. Approx. Theory 30 (1980), 81 - 98.

KARTSATOS, A.G. and SAFF, E.B. [73]: Hyperpolynomial approximation of solutions of nonlinear integro-differential equations. Pacific J. of Math. 49 (1973), 117 - 125.

KNABNER, P. [83]: Stability theorems for general free boundary problems of the Stefan type and applications. In "Applied nonlinear Functional-analysis" (R. Gorenflo, K.-H. Hoffmann, Eds.), pp. 95 - 116, Peter Lang, Frankfurt/Bern, 1983.

KNABNER, P. [83a]: Fragen der Rekonstruktion und der Steuerung bei Stefan Problemen und ihre Behandlung über lineare Ersatzaufgaben. Dissertation, Augsburg, 1983.

KNABNER, P. [85]: Control of Stefan problems by means of linear-quadratic defect minimization. Numer. Math. 46 (1985), 429 - 442.

KRABS, W. [73]: Stabilität und Stetigkeit bei nichtlinearer Optimierung. In "Operations Research-Verfahren XVII" (R. Henn et al., Eds.), pp. 207 - 228, Verlag Anton Hain, Meisenheim, 1973.

KRABS, W. [73a]: Discretization of approximation problems in the view of optimization. In "Approximation theory" (G.G. Lorentz, Ed.), pp. 395 - 401, Academic Press, New York/London, 1973.

KRABS, W. [73b]: On discretization in generalized rational approximation. In "Abhandlungen aus dem Mathematischen Seminar der Universität Hamburg" (R. Ansorge et al., Eds.), vol. 39, pp. 231 - 244, Vandenhoeck & Ruprecht, Göttingen, 1973.

KRABS, W. [77]: Stetige Abänderung der Daten bei nichtlinearer Optimierung und ihre Konsequenzen. In "Operations Research-Verfahren XXV" (R. Henn et al., Eds.), pp. 93 - 113, Verlag Anton Hain, Meisenheim, 1977.

KRABS, W. [79]: Optimization and Approximation. John Wiley & Sons, Chichester/New York/Brisbane/Toronto, 1979.

KRABS, W. [79a]: Optimal error estimates for linear operator equations. In "Numerical Mathematics" (R. Ansorge et al., Eds.), ISNM 49, pp. 97 - 106, Birkhäuser, Basel/Boston/Stuttgart, 1979.

KROÓ, A. [81]: Best L_1-approximation on finite point sets: rate of convergence. J. Approx. Theory 33 (1981), 340 - 352.

KRUEGER, H. [82]: Zum Newtonverfahren für ein Stefanproblem. In "Numerical treatment of free boundary problems" (J. Albrecht et al., Eds.), ISNM 58, pp. 245 - 253, Birkhäuser Verlag, Basel/Boston/Stuttgart, 1982.

LADYŽENSKAJA, O.A., Ed., [67]: Boundary value problems of mathematical physics III. Proceedings of the Steklov Institute of Mathematics 83 (1965), translated by American Mathematical Society, Providence, R.I., 1967.

LOEB, H.L. and WOLFE, J.M. [73]: Discrete nonlinear approximation. J. Approx. Theory 7 (1973), 365 - 385.

McEWEN, W.H. [31]: Problems of closest approximation connected with the solution of linear differential equations. Trans. Amer. Math. Soc. 33 (1931), 979 - 997.

MEIRMANOV, A.M. [81]: On the classical solution of the multidimensional Stefan problem for quasilinear parabolic equations. Math. USSR Sbornik 40 (1981), 157 - 178.

OBERG, E.N. [35]: The approximate solution of integral equations. Bull. Amer. Math. Soc. 41 (1935), 276 - 284.

PETSOULAS, A.G. [75]: The approximate solution of Volterra integral equations. J. Approx. Theory 14 (1975), 152 - 159.

PUCCI, C. [59]: Alcune limitazioni per le soluzioni di equazioni paraboliche. Ann. di Matematica 48 (1959), 161 - 172.

RABINOWITZ, P. [68]: Applications of linear programming to numerical analysis. SIAM Review 10 (1968), 121 - 159.

REEMTSEN, R. [80]: On level sets and an approximation problem for the numerical solution of a free boundary problem. Computing 27 (1980), 27 - 35.

REEMTSEN, R. [82]: On the convergence of a class of nonlinear approximation methods. J. Approx. Theory 36 (1982), 237 - 256.

REEMTSEN, R. [82a]: The method of minimizing the defects for the Stefan problem. In "Numerical treatment of free boundary problems" (J. Albrecht et al., Eds.), ISNM 58, pp. 245 - 253, Birkhäuser Verlag, Basel/Boston/Stuttgart, 1982.

REEMTSEN, R. [87]: On discretization errors in nonlinear approximation problems. J. Approx. Theory, to appear, 1987.

REEMTSEN, R. and KIRSCH, A. [82]: A method for the numerical solution of the one-dimensional inverse Stefan problem, Part II. Preprint Nr. 652, TH Darmstadt, 1982.

REEMTSEN, R. and KIRSCH, A. [84]: A method for the numerical solution of the one-dimensional inverse Stefan problem. Numer. Math. 45 (1984), 253 - 273.

REEMTSEN, R. and LOZANO, C. [81]: An approximation technique for the numerical solution of a Stefan problem. Numer. Math. 38 (1981), 141 - 154.

ROCKAFELLAR, R.T. [72]: Convex analysis. Princeton Univ. Press, Princeton, N.J., 1972.

RUBINSTEIN, L., FASANO, A., and PRIMICERIO, M. [80]: Remarks on the analyticity of the free boundary for the one-dimensional Stefan problem. Ann. di Mat. Pura et Appl. 125 (1980), 295 - 311.

SCHABACK, R. [84]: Numerische Approximation. NAM-Bericht 45, Universität Göttingen, 1 - 69, 1984.

SCHABACK, R. [85]: Convergence analysis of the general Gauss-Newton algorithm. Numer. Math. 46 (1985), 281 - 309.

SCHMIDT, D. and WIGGINS, K.L. [79]: Minimax approximate solutions of linear boundary value problems. Math. of Comp. 33 (1979), 139 - 148.

SHERMAN, B. [71]: Free boundary problems for the heat equation in which the moving interface coincides initially with the fixed face. J. Math. Anal. Appl. 33 (1971), 449 - 466.

STEIN, F.M. and KLOPFENSTEIN, K.F. [68]: Approximate solutions of a system of differential equations. J. Approx. Theory 1 (1968), 279 - 292.

STERNBERG, W. [29]: Über die Gleichung der Wärmeleitung. Math. Ann. 101 (1929), 394 - 398.

STUMMEL, F. [73]: Approximation methods in analysis. Lecture Notes Ser. No. 35, Mat. Inst., Aarhus Universitet, 1973.

VAINIKKO, G. [76]: Funktionalanalysis der Diskretisierungsmethoden. Teubner Verlagsgesellschaft, Leipzig, 1976.

WALTER, W. [72]: Gewöhnliche Differentialgleichungen. Springer Verlag, Berlin/Heidelberg/New York, 1972.

WATSON, G.A. [80]: Approximation theory and numerical methods. John Wiley & Sons, Chichester/New York/Brisbane/Toronto, 1980.

WENDLAND, W.L. [79]: Elliptic systems in the plane. Pitman, London/ San Francisco/Melbourne, 1979.

WIDDER, D.V. [75]: The heat equation. Academic Press, New York/San Francisco/ London, 1975.

WIGGINS, K.L. [78]: Successive approximations to solutions of Volterra integral equations. J. Approx. Theory 22 (1978), 340 - 349.

WIGGINS, K.L. [79]: Best L_p approximate solutions of nonlinear integro-differential equations. J. Approx. Theory 26 (1979), 329 - 339.

WOLFE, J.M. [75]: Discrete rational L_p approximation. Maths. of Comp. 29 (1975), 540 - 548.

WOLFE, J.M. [77]: Existence and convergence of discrete nonlinear best L_2 approximations. J. Approx. Theory 20 (1977), 1 - 9.

WOLFE, J.M. [79]: Convergence of discrete rational approximations. J. Approx. Theory 27 (1979), 271 - 277.

YOUNG, J.W. [07]: General theory of approximation by functions involving a given number of arbitrary parameters. Trans. Am. Math. Soc. 23 (1907), 331 - 344.